READING, WRITING, & INQUIRY

in the SCIENCE CLASSROOM

Grades 6–12

READING, WRITING, & INQUIRY

in the SCIENCE CLASSROOM

Grades 6–12

Strategies to Improve Content Learning

Kathleen Chamberlain • Christine Corby Crane

CORWIN PRESS
A SAGE Company

For information:

Corwin Press
A SAGE Company
2455 Teller Road
Thousand Oaks, California 91320
www.corwinpress.com

SAGE Ltd.
1 Oliver's Yard
55 City Road
London, EC1Y 1SP
United Kingdom

SAGE India Pvt. Ltd.
B 1/I 1 Mohan Cooperative
  Industrial Area
Mathura Road, New Delhi 110044
India

SAGE Asia-Pacific Pte. Ltd.
33 Pekin Street #02–01
Far East Square
Singapore 048763

Printed in the United States of America.

Library of Congress Cataloging-in-Publication Data

Chamberlain, Kathleen, 1948–
 Reading, writing, and inquiry in the science classroom, grades 6–12 : strategies to improve content learning / Kathleen Chamberlain, Christine Corby Crane.
     p. cm.
 Includes bibliographical references and index.
 ISBN 978-1-4129-6070-0 (cloth : acid-free paper)
 ISBN 978-1-4129-6071-7 (pbk. : acid-free paper)
 1. Science—Study and teaching (Elementary) 2. Science—Study and teaching (Secondary) I. Crane, Christine Corby. II. Title.

LB1585.C424 2009
 372.35'044–dc22

2008020178

This book is printed on acid-free paper.

08 09 10 11 10 9 8 7 6 5 4 3 2 1

Acquisitions Editor: Cathy Hernandez
Editorial Assistants: Ena Rosen and Megan Bedell
Production Editor: Appingo Publishing Services
Cover Designer: Scott Van Atta

Contents

List of Figures

Preface

At the national and state levels, reading and writing across the curriculum are being promoted—and in some cases required. As we began this project, we had two questions: Why should reading, writing, and inquiry be included in a secondary science classroom? How can this be done? We each have our own area of interest—inquiry-based science or literacy in secondary classrooms—and have taught corresponding undergraduate and graduate courses. Combined, we have more years in classroom teaching than we wish to count. Yet we both became learners during the development of this book. We talked to classroom teachers and to our colleagues. We explained and clarified our own ideas and challenged each other's assertions. As we worked together, we shared information and blended methods in our effort to present theoretically based, yet practical, ideas that could be used in secondary classrooms. We hope our readers will join us in our learning experience. The role of reading, writing, and literacy in science classrooms is evolving. Many of the ideas in this book come from classroom experiences—our own and those of our colleagues. We encourage readers to try these ideas or develop your own.

According to Chiappetta and Koballa (2002), four elements should be integrated into science lessons:

Science as a Belief

Some beliefs have changed over time with new discoveries. Six characteristics that mold belief include:

- *Curiosity*—Scientists ask questions. Some scientists are so driven to prove their ideas that they may be ridiculed, discriminated against, or persecuted for their beliefs.
- *Imagination*—Scientific and technological knowledge has its roots in imagination.
- *Reasoning*—Looking at patterns in nature and collection of data through observation and experimentation help scientists obtain knowledge.
- *Cause and effect*—Such relationships prompt many "why" questions that scientists seek to answer.
- *Belief and rejection*—How do we know what to believe or not believe?
- *Attitude*—Scientists need to be open minded and objective when seeking facts.

Science Investigation

There are many facets of scientific investigation and no specific format for procedure. However, there are three aspects that need to be included:

- *Hypothesis*—We state an educated guess of what is the cause of or reason for something that will be tested.
- *Experimentation*—Using controls shows relationships among variables that can be changed. One must be careful because data can be manipulated to produce false beliefs.
- *Observation*—The use of senses helps to obtain observations resulting from our experimentation.

Science Knowledge

- *Facts* are based on observations and can be demonstrated at any time.
- *Concepts, principles,* and *laws* must be meaningful to the learner after having opportunities to explore. They tie together facts.
- *Theories* are used as tentative explanations until proven otherwise.
- *Models* are useful to help explain a concept but are not exact.

Science, Technology, and Society

- *Technology* includes highly sophisticated instruments to help solve problems.
- *Society* is impacted by science and supplies support and funds for projects.

If these elements are to be included into a science lesson, how do we combine them with reading, writing, and technology? Richard Preston (1996), in the foreword of his book *First Light*, states:

Scientific facts are often described in textbooks as if they just sort of exist, like nickels someone picked up on the street. But science at the cutting edge, conducted by sharp minds probing deep into nature, is not about self-evident facts. It is about mystery and not knowing. It is about taking huge risks. It is about wasting time, getting burned, and failing. It is like trying to crack a monstrous safe that has a complicated, secret lock. . . . Sometimes there is a faint clicking sound, and the door pulls wide open, and you walk in. (pp. xiii–xiv)

Is he saying we must take risks to encourage the sharp minds of students—to let them take risks—and hope that the door to science will open for them? Can teachers take risks and incorporate different approaches that encourage students to enjoy the mystery of science and to think like scientists, act like scientists, and gain scientific knowledge which they may be able to understand, apply, and communicate with others? Inquiry-based science may provide a means to that end.

Inquiry-based science has been promoted by national-level organizations such as the American Association for the Advancement of Science (AAAS) and the National Science Teachers Association. According to the *National Science Education Standards* (National Research Council, 1996), there are five elements of science inquiry:

- Scientifically oriented questions
- Priority of evidence
- Formulation of explanations from evidence
- Connecting explanations to scientific knowledge
- Communicating and justifying conclusions

Conversations with preservice and practicing teachers suggest that of the five essential elements, those that appear to be the most difficult to implement in lessons are developing questions, connecting explanations to scientific knowledge, and communicating and justifying conclusions. We searched through literature by and about scientists; we were particularly interested in how scientists defined literacy. The above elements are related to science literacy.

Jennifer Cartier and Jim Stewart (2000) provide an overview of a high school genetics inquiry-based unit in an article you can find in *Science and Education*. In that article, they state that those who are scientifically literate "possess familiarity with key scientific concepts and an ability to relate those concepts to their everyday lives in decision-making or problem-solving situations" (p. 249). Cartier and Stewart reference reading materials that can be used to understand how ideas have historically developed and give examples of materials that students are required to read, such as a revised version of Mendel's work. They also give examples of writing students must do in the unit, including keeping a notebook of their ideas and experiences and journaling. Articles such as this support our assumptions that reading and writing could be effectively included.

Chapter 1 begins our exploration by addressing foundational assumptions about the meaning of literacy, specifically science literacy, and the meaning of inquiry-based science. The chapter describes lesson designs that are models for inquiry.

Chapter 2 introduces reading as it relates to science education and addresses the relationship of textbooks to inquiry-based instruction. Strategies that are presented that support student comprehension of written material are ones that may be adopted for many types of reading materials.

Chapter 3 continues the discussion of reading through the use of nontextbook materials. These two chapters support the fourth element of inquiry as presented above—students seek to verify or confirm their conclusions by comparing their results to what they have encountered in literature and to existing scientific knowledge.

Chapter 4 addresses the fifth element, communication, by presenting strategies for writing in the science classroom. It discusses the specifics of scientific writing compared and contrasted to other types of writing. We present the

Science Writing Heuristic, which is intended to guide students as they construct knowledge through inquiry, thus using writing to learn.

Chapter 5 shows how technology can be used to enhance students' science knowledge as they define problems, collect and analyze data, and communicate their knowledge to others. The chapter connects technological literacy to reading, writing, and inquiry. We discuss how students can be encouraged to use and evaluate resources available to them over the Internet and show similarities to strategies used when reading. We also provide resources available for teachers to use.

Our goal was to develop material that will aid teachers who are beginning to use inquiry-based methods and those who have already begun to use inquiry and wish to expand or refine their teaching methods. We hope to meet the needs of secondary classroom teachers who are being encouraged to incorporate more reading and writing in their lessons. Because students in classrooms are becoming more diverse and teachers are being asked to work with students with many different needs, we have included ideas that can be used with struggling students and students who need enrichment. We encourage readers to use the materials we present as a catalyst for developing their own strategies and as a vehicle for conversation with others.

Acknowledgments

We would like to thank our husbands, Bill Chamberlain and John Crane, for their support for our professional lives. They put up with our times away from home, take-out meals, and books and papers stacked everywhere. Without them, we would not have been able to accomplish our goals.

We would also like to thank the many other professionals we have met during our careers who have shared their ideas and struggles. Some of the strategies and activities included in this book are original or from our "stashes" of materials we accumulated during our careers. We have made every attempt to track down original sources for ideas. If we were not able to find original sources and inadvertently did not give proper credit, please let us know. We will make corrections in future publications.

PUBLISHER'S ACKNOWLEDGMENTS

Corwin Press gratefully acknowledges the contributions of the following reviewers:

Richard Cash
Gifted and Talented Department
Bloomington Public Schools
Bloomington, MN

Randy Cook
Chemistry Teacher
Tri-CountyHigh School
Morley, MI

Lisa Edwards
Science Teacher
Hickory High School
Hickory, NC

Jane Hunn
Science Teacher
Tippecanoe Valley Middle School
Akron, IN

Sharon Kane
Professor of Curriculum and Instruction
State University of New York at Oswego
Oswego, NY

Gail Marshall
Professor of Curriculum and Instruction
University of West Georgia
Carrollton, GA

Charre Todd
Science Teacher
Norman Junior High School
Crossett, AR

Gary L. Willhite
Reading and Language Studies
KDP Co-Counselor
Southern Illinois University
Carbondale, IL

About the Authors

 **Kathleen Chamberlain, PhD,** recently retired from Lycoming College in Williamsport, Pennsylvania, where she was an assistant professor of education and taught courses in curriculum and instruction, educational foundations, and literacy for secondary certification. While at Lycoming, she also served as Assistant Dean for Teaching Effectiveness. She is a former teacher and administrator in K–12 schools. She received her doctorate in Curriculum and Instruction from Pennsylvania State University, where she focused on middle-level education and school communities. A graduate of Indiana University of Pennsylvania, she earned her Master's of Science in Education from Mansfield University of Pennsylvania. She has Pennsylvania administrative certifications from Bucknell University. Dr. Chamberlain is the author of *Middle Schools for a Diverse Society* (2003) and also journal articles about middle schools and science education and has conducted numerous workshops about teaching strategies, literacy, and student assessment. Currently, she is conducting research with a school administrator in a consortium of school districts that deals with addiction-prevention programs for adolescents. In addition to work, she enjoys living in Delaware, her family, writing, and quilting.

 **Christine Corby Crane, PhD,** recently retired from the Athens Area School District in Athens, Pennsylvania, after teaching 26 years. She was the K–12 Science Department chair for the Athens Area School District for 9 years. She was instrumental in the district obtaining Pennsylvania Environment and Ecology Exemplary Status for the 2007 school year after obtaining three grants to develop and implement a curriculum involving the Chesapeake Bay Watershed. In addition to teaching in Athens, she was an associate professor at Mansfield University, teaching science and technology methods courses, and has taught K–12 science education courses for Penn State University. She has been a consultant for several federal, state, and community science education programs. She received her doctorate in Curriculum and Instruction from Pennsylvania State University, where she focused on science education and language and literacy. A graduate of Elmira College, she earned her Master's of Science from Mansfield University of Pennsylvania. Dr. Crane contributed to the *Pennsylvania Department of Energy Elementary Energy and Environment Science Activities, Volume VI*, and she is also the coauthor of a journal article, "Middle School Students Perceptions on How They Learn Science; Support for Inquiry-Based Classrooms." She conducts workshops and presentations on teaching science. She teaches undergraduate courses and graduate science education courses as an adjunct professor at local colleges. In addition to her educational endeavors, she enjoys spending time with family and friends.

Inquiry and Scientific Literacy

WHAT IS SCIENCE?

How do you define science? How do you think your students define science, or how would they describe a scientist? Not too long ago, we had a group of seventh-grade students draw scientists. Overwhelmingly, the pictures depicted men (some with Einstein-like hair) standing behind lab tables using flasks or test tubes. The average person might define science as a body of scientific knowledge. Philosophers may regard science as a means to obtain the truth through questioning, while scientists probably see science as a means of exploring a hypothesis by following a set of procedures. In a classroom, the teacher may encourage students to think of science as problem solving, observation and description of the real world, discovery, seeking the truth, studying nature, turning facts into theories, organizing knowledge, using logic, or studying the universe.

While all of these statements have a connection with science, each is only a part of science—only when they are put together do they begin to represent science. Science is learning about the world. All dimensions of science rather than an emphasis on only science content, support this learning. Knowledge is obtained through observations and investigations that can be substantiated by others. According to the National Research Council (NRC; 1999), explanations that cannot be based on empirical evidence are not part of science. Science is one subject that encourages concrete action (Wright & Wright, 1998).

There are three aspects of science knowledge for which scientists are responsible—*understand, explain,* and *apply.* Careful observations, designed experimentation, and logical reasoning can accomplish these aspects. Scientists are also responsible for making understandings public. Generally, scientists make these public at professional meetings or in journals. Other scientists then carefully review these understandings, making critical comments and suggestions (Chiappetta & Koballa, 2002). Students who are scientifically literate are able to not only follow scientific procedures, but they also understand, explain, and apply their knowledge.

WHAT IS SCIENTIFIC LITERACY?

According to the NRC (1996), a scientifically literate individual is able to

- experience the satisfaction of understanding the natural world;
- use scientific thinking in making personal decisions;
- participate intelligently in societal discussions on science and technology; and
- attain the skills and knowledge that are required for being productive in our current and future economies. (p. 13)

The characteristics of a scientific literate adult include being able to use clear and accurate communications skills determining differences between vague and unsubstantiated arguments with possible and relevant ones (American Association for the Advancement of Science [AAAS], 1993). People need to be able to apply problem-solving skills to everyday life (Wright & Wright, 1998).

While scientific knowledge is dependent upon texts, DeBoer (2000) noted that being able to read and write about science is rather broad and is not necessarily being scientifically literate. Just being able to memorize vocabulary is NOT being scientifically literate (Norris & Phillips, 2003). Students need to understand the vocabulary allowing them to read alternative views in articles and comprehending science ideas in the media (Miller, 1998).

There are obstacles that interfere with scientific literacy. Rather than teach in an inquiry fashion to promote scientific literacy, critics assert that students are being taught in preparation for standardized testing (Bentley, Ebert, & Ebert, 2002; Grossen, Romance, & Vitale, 1994; Rescher, 2000). On the other hand, others claim that science teachers have little or no concern for reading in science and do not see reading as an important part of science (Wellington & Osborne, 2001). To further complicate matters, while science departments are made up of qualified teachers who are socially respectful of each other, often there is little or no collaboration among departments. Not only is science taught separately from other academic areas, but it is also divided into separate compartments within its own department (Rubin & Wilson, 2001). How much more beneficial science and literature education could be if they were brought together by creating experiences where students use principles, theories, and generalizations from both academic areas to solve a particular problem or explore an area of interest (Howes, Hamilton, & Zaskoda, 2003).

Learning science is a personal and social exploration that promotes conceptual change. For there to be true science literacy, experiences must incorporate scientific inquiry and self-discovery (Wright & Wright, 1998). The more direct the student involvement, the better the experience is (King, 2007). Throughout this book, we hope to provide readers with ideas to increase science literacy through curriculum not traditionally associated with science—reading and writing.

HOW DO WE REACH
SCIENTIFIC LITERACY?

There are many options for improvement in science education for high school students. Many contemporary reform ideas are based on advances in cognitive psychology and human development research (Wandersee, Mintzes, & Novak, 1998). As a result, the *National Science Education Standards* were developed to provide curriculum and instructional guidelines for all students that describe what students and teachers need to know in order to promote a science-literate society. States have implemented their own standards based on these national standards. Teachers and science curriculum coordinators need to be aware of their state's science standards to ensure that the standards are better met (NRC, 1996). As the final arbiters of any reform, teachers' perceptions about reform ideals are worthy of investigation (Crane, 1998). There is no single curriculum adequate for all students. Some have even turned students off science. Curriculum designers must take care to not adopt any one wholesale package program (Airasian & Walsh, 1997; Nordstrom, 1992).

Learners involved with a process of inquiry that allows them to answer questions that challenge their prior knowledge about themselves, the world around them, and the environment are growing in science literacy and knowledge. Students can then restructure their informal ideas to those consistent with the science community (Driver, Asoko, Leach, Mortimer, & Scott, 1994). Unfortunately, in many science classrooms, inquiry has not achieved primacy over the traditional teaching method. Bentley and Alouf (2003) determined that

> While leaders in the field of science education and science teacher educators continue to promote inquiry teaching, traditional didactic expository instructional methods; such as teacher-centered whole-class lecture and textbook-based read-about-science activities still make up much of the science instruction in American classrooms. (p. 3)

The environment found in an inquiry-based science classroom may blossom from the different abilities, attitudes, experiences, and interests that students bring. Mary Ellsworth (2002), model teacher for the Gallaudet University Model Secondary School for the Deaf in Washington, D.C., suggests that many teachers do not know the value of using activity-based activities with deaf students. We suggest that activity-based science has application for all students, including those with disabilities.

Good science inquiry involves learning through direct interaction with materials and a phenomenon (Kluger-Bell, 2000). It involves making observations, posing questions and researching with books and other resources to enhance what is already known, planning investigations to solve problems, and comparing what is already known along with the investigation's experimental evidence. It is important to use current scientific knowledge and understanding to guide the scientific investigation. Inquiry uses tools to gather, analyze, and interpret data. Technology used to collect the data can enhance the amount of data, the speed with which it can be collected, and potentially the accuracy allowing the investigator to analyze and quantify the results. Communicating the results concludes the research. Researchers need to propose answers, explanations, and predictions throughout the investigation and use critical and logical thinking, identify assumptions, and consider alternative explanations. It is because of these last three activities that science distinguishes itself from other ways of knowing and provides for the best possible explanations of the natural world.

One of the benefits of inquiry-based instruction that has been observed is enhanced students' performances in laboratory skills and interpreting data (Mattheis & Nakayama, 1988). An inquiry-based classroom promotes critical-thinking skills. It empowers students to become independent and lifelong learners (Llewellyn, 2005). According to Regan, Case, and Brubacker (2000, p. 2), "inquiry-based classrooms promote critical thinking skills and habits of mind."

To urge educators to promote broader objectives in education, Ferrero (2005, p. 425) expanded on the four NRC (1999) principles necessary in a learning environment. He stated that

- Schools and classrooms could be learner centered with students setting their own learning by means of consulting with peers as well as the teacher.
- To ensure that students understand information and subject matter, classrooms should be knowledge centered with students knowing why it is important to know what is being taught.
- Assessments should be ongoing with both teachers and students guiding instruction and monitoring progress.
- There should be a strong sense of community with focus on career and connections to the outside world that help prepare students to identify social injustice and organize for political action.

Science, Technology, and Society (STS) programs have been particularly successful because topics are frequently related to students' lives. Activities are often conducted by groups, and there are often connections to other school subjects. Teachers who guide students to make connections with other subjects help the students go beyond learning isolated facts. Students can focus on processes for learning. Students who have difficulty in some areas often become problem solvers and have learned to develop other skills. Learning can be enhanced by tapping into these other learning modes (Caseau & Norman, 1997).

STS activities may help students identify with the science they are learning in their classrooms. Additionally, their environments and personal issues may provide an opportunity to develop questions for inquiry. By being aware of students' lives outside of school, teachers and curriculum developers may make decisions that provide for relevant and motivational learning experiences.

CLASSROOM STRATEGIES

We tend to teach the way we personally learn and often must make a determined effort to consider our students' preferences. Students learn better and enjoy their learning activities more when the teaching style closely matches their learning styles (She, 2005). It is beyond the scope of our discussion here to spend an inordinate amount of time on the many different learning-style theories. These theories can be synthesized into identifying three different kinds of learners—visual, auditory, and kinesthetic. Between 30% and 35% of students are probably visual learners. They relate to pictures more than words; they would rather view materials than read them. They learn vocabulary in context after having opportunities to hear the words. They use visual cues in texts; graphic organizers help them comprehend material. Approximately the same percentage are tactile-kinesthetic learners. They look at such things as the shape of words and understand concepts better if they have concrete examples at the beginning of the learning experience. Auditory learners like to hear and talk about their learning (Winebrenner, 1996). With so many different students, we can't be expected to meet every student's learning style every day. Instead, throughout a unit of study, we can include activities related to a variety of learning styles.

Most secondary classroom strategies fall into categories. According to Chiappetta and Koballa (2002) the strategies include *lectures* during which teachers present ideas to a large group of students. In these situations, there is little student involvement. *Discussions* allow students to clarify ideas; however, unless the discussions are carefully designed, teachers often do most of the talking, and student willingness to participate may vary according to the classroom climate. *Demonstrations* usually have minimal student participation but do help teachers explain ideas and guide thinking. *Laboratory* or *hands-on activities* are usually predictable and prearranged by the teacher. However, they may be designed to encourage process skills, inductive reasoning, or deductive reasoning. *Simulations* and *games* help students visualize events or objects they might otherwise not have the opportunity to experience. The availability of technology allows for rich learning experiences for students in many classrooms. The final strategy as outlined in Chiappetta and Koballa's work is *recitation*. While this does involve student participation, it is usually teacher directed and deals with rote memory of knowledge.

Inquiry, as recommended by Project 2061 of the AAAS (1993) engages students with productive questions, prompting them to become actively engaged in seeking a solution. Students are encouraged to work in cooperative groups testing ideas, collecting data, forming conclusions based on the evidence obtained, and communicating results. Teachers are encouraged to deemphasize rote memorization of vocabulary (Chiappetta & Koballa, 2002).

Teaching science by inquiry allows students to perform investigations using skills used by scientists. Productive questions to guide students from recitation of facts to being able to apply knowledge in new situations and then to making evaluations based upon knowledge promotes thinking. Students should be engaged in science process skills such as observation, classification, measurement, mathematic calculations, making predictions, and designing investigations through the manipulation of controls. Use of these skills helps students become better problem solvers (Chiappetta & Koballa, 2002).

How are you smart? We're not asking how smart you are. What are you really good at doing? Look at your students. Do you have natural leaders, quiet thinkers, sports jocks, and artists? According to a theory proposed by Howard Gardner, there are at least eight "intelligences" or ways of being smart and we all have each of the intelligences in some degree. Multiple Intelligences theory has the potential to enhance conceptual understanding in science, foster positive attitudes toward science, increase enjoyment of and participation in science, and create more authentic learning experience in science (Goodnough, 2001; Thompson & MacDougall, 2002). If we design units during which many of the intelligences are addressed, students will not only have an opportunity to participate in an area of strength, but will also be challenged to expand their capabilities in other areas. For example, an inquiry unit that includes reading, field studies, problem solving in groups, an oral presentation with visual aids designed by students, and individual logs and reflections can meet the needs of a variety of students.

Figure 1.1   Howard Gardner's Intelligences

Verbal-linguistic—These are your students who are good talkers, readers, and writers.

Mathematical/Logical—These are your analytic thinkers who are comfortable with if . . . then statements and calculations.

Musical—These students are musical, and they are also those who can sense rhythms in nature or their environments.

Visual/Spatial—These students are your artists, ones who can organize space around them. They can visualize quantities and volumes.

Interpersonal—These are the students who work well in groups; they are often your leaders.

Intrapersonal—These students are your quiet thinkers; they may be shy and reluctant to speak out, but actually think things through and may come up with great ideas.

Bodily Kinesthetic—These students are physically aware and enjoy working with their hands and bodies.

Naturalist—These students are keenly aware of their environment. They can easily distinguish between different species or even the kinds of cars they see on the road.

SOURCE: Adapted from Manner, B. M. (2001). Learning styles and multiple intelligences in students: Getting the most out of your students' learning. *Journal of College Science Teaching, 30*(6), 390–393.

Discrepancies between goals for student achievement and what we actually see happening suggest that one-size-fits-all strategies are not the answer. Perhaps, in addition to identifying the features of materials that are not working, we should consider the needs and abilities of the students. Students may have different goals—some actually anti-achievement goals—that may be based upon their backgrounds, interests, and abilities (Chamberlain, 2003). Inquiry-based science can help students identify goals and work toward achieving these goals.

Mastropieri and Scruggs (1992) suggest that the characteristics of science make science classes appropriate for inclusion of students with special needs. They suggest that the experiential hands-on approach can help develop skills and knowledge necessary for adult life. Experiences in science can help students develop problem-solving and decision-making skills. Although including students with exceptionalities may require some modifications of classroom procedures and strategies, students benefit from access to the same curriculum as other students and the opportunities for social interactions and friendships with their peers (Mastropieri & Scruggs, 2001).

Because science provides an opportunity for students to "develop reasoning skills and apply the scientific 'process' skills . . . to phenomena they encounter in their everyday lives" (Scruggs, Mastropieri, & Wolfe, 1995, p. 223), it is an important subject for students with mental retardation. Activity-based learning allows students to interact with phenomena and to manipulate equipment and materials. Practice with decision making and problem solving helps students achieve academic and social goals (Caseau & Norman, 1997).

Most of the students included in regular classes with individualized education plans (IEPs) will be labeled *learning disabled* (LD). However, this category is wide and has many variations. The common characteristic of students with learning disabilities is that a student is at or above average in general intellectual ability, but there are discrepancies in achievement among different academic areas. For instance, a student may have high achievement in mathematics but have difficulty reading. Individual students may have difficulty reading, expressing thoughts in writing or orally, or difficulty with focusing on tasks or calculations. Students with learning disabilities may exhibit inappropriate social behavior either from self-consciousness regarding academic deficiencies or from inappropriate interpretation of social cues. A student with a history of school failure or underachievement can be expected to lack motivation for future school tasks and may have attention problems (Scruggs & Mastropieri, 1993). Students with learning disabilities may require fewer accommodations in science classes that are well structured and activity based than in any other academic subject. In fact, classes that are well structured and activity based are particularly helpful to students with a learning disability (Caseau & Norman, 1997). Only careful scrutiny of a student's IEP and consultations with special educators familiar with the student can identify adaptations that may be required in the classroom.

A student's success is directly related to how the student sees himself or herself as a learner and how the student defines success. Success in science is also determined by how well the curriculum matches the needs of students—developmentally, culturally, and academically (Chamberlain, 2003). Inquiry-based science can be a vehicle to meet the challenges of diversity among students and the need for science literacy in a changing society. The task is not easy, but it is worth the effort. The National Science Teachers Association's 2004 position statement supports the inclusion of special students in science. The organization's

Web site (www.nsta.org), which provides background information and suggested strategies for many disabilities, is an excellent resource for teachers. The suggestions are practical and easy to use; they mirror many of the strategies already presented in this book. There are also other organizations that provide information for teachers. On the Rochester Institute of Technology's Web site (www.rit.edu), teachers can find information about the Clearinghouse on Mathematics, Engineering, Technology, and Science (COMETS) program; the site has many suggestions and provides support for those working with students who have hearing impairments.

QUESTIONING

We keep mentioning questions—student and teacher posed—that guide inquiry. Well-designed questions focus attention and help students move beyond facts to understanding and application. The lowest level of questions requires recitation of information students have acquired from sources. These literal questions encourage students to search for facts. Although facts may be important, questions that require students to make inferences, connect information, and apply information to new situations are necessary. At the highest level of questioning, the critical level, students are required to evaluate information, to challenge information by comparing several sources of information, and to use information to support conclusions (Gabler & Schroeder, 2003).

If the goal of a question is to focus students on facts or observations, one may use phrases such as "how many . . . " or "what happened when. . . ." However, to move students to higher thinking, use questions that require students to compare and contrast ideas or results. Ask students "what if . . . " or "how could we . . . " or give reasons and explain phenomena. It may be necessary to start with lower-level questioning and guide students to more inquiry-focused questions. However, open-ended questions, ones that do not have just one right answer, are most productive in inquiry-focused science.

INQUIRY TEACHING MODELS

The most widely promoted approach to science instruction today is constructivism, which holds that knowledge is constructed within the human minds and social communities (Richardson, 1999). The teacher is no longer the controller of students (Tobin & Dawson, 1992). Learning is built upon knowledge from previous experiences, feelings, and skills. While constructivism does not neglect basic skills, it emphasizes thinking, reasoning, and applying knowledge (Moussiaux & Norman, 2005). Misconceptions are common and sometimes interfere with learning if students resist changing their own ideas (Schulte, 1996). Once learners assimilate or acquire new ideas to replace their old conceptions with new ones, then accommodation occurs. This happens when the learner becomes dissatisfied with existing conceptions (Wandersee et al., 1998). Often, a lot of time in science classrooms is spent on helping students take in new information, but often with little attention to helping them learn to apply this information in real-life situations.

Students do not simply learn by listening to someone talk or by reading a textbook (Rakow, 1998). If students know the teacher will be testing on factual aspects of a reading assignment, they will adopt an apathetic stance, seeking only the factual information in their reading assignment (Rosenblatt, 1991). Mayer (1995) noted that this form of reading may actually interfere with the science process. Textbooks and illustrations may confuse students' understanding of concepts. Suggestions to help overcome these problems when using textbooks will be discussed in Chapter 2.

The constructivist model of learning is reflected in inquiry-based instruction and is characterized in a variety of ways (Collins, 1986; DeBoer, 1991). Teachers and students become partners in learning with students having a role in producing knowledge, not just receiving it from the teacher (Haury, 1993). Students are capable of providing insight into the effectiveness of curriculum (Chamberlain, 1999). Students are more apt to understand the natural world if they are given the opportunity to use their senses to directly observe natural phenomena. Sometimes scientific instruments are needed to extend the power of their senses (National Science Board, 1991).

5E Model for Lesson Design

The 5E Model is made up of five distinct parts and can be an extremely effective learning approach (Guzzetti, Taylor, Glass, & Gammas, 1993; Lawson, 1995). This model gives students the opportunity to raise questions and put abstract experiences in communicable form. They can expand on previously learned concepts making the connection to other concepts. This, in turn, leads to further inquiry and new understandings (not to answers, but more questions). The five parts of this lesson design are:

1. **Engage**—During this segment of the lesson, the intent is to capture students' interest, get them thinking about the subject matter, and stimulate their thinking.

2. **Explore**—Students are given the opportunity to design and implement their own investigation. Through observations, forming hypotheses, recording data, organizing their findings, creating graphs, and other forms of communicating their results, students then share their findings.

3. **Explain**—The teacher introduces facts, models, laws, and theories to the students during this phase. Students are helped with scientific vocabulary and guided in formulating questions to help them explain the results of their exploration.

4. **Elaborate**—At this point of the model, a transfer of learning from one concept to another should take place with students applying their new knowledge.

5. **Evaluate**—Students and teachers conduct assessments that are not only formative but are also summative of students' learning.

Teachers also look for understanding during the Explore and Explain phases. According to Colburn and Clough (1997), students can design experiments as part of their assessment. They can also create explanations and demonstrations of their knowledge. It is extremely important for students to have adequate time to discuss their findings, present their data, and listen to what is presented by others, as it is crucial to improve retention of the knowledge and concepts gained through the initial inquiry.

7E Model (An Expansion of the 5E)

Arthur Eisenkraft (2003), project director of the Active Physics program, expanded on the 5E by adding two additional phases. He divided the Engage phase to include an Elicit phase. While it is important to engage students in inquiry, it is also important for the teacher to understand students' prior knowledge. This can be accomplished by asking productive questions that elicit students' understanding about a concept. Eisenkraft also added the Extend phase at the end, which allows students to challenge what they have already learned. Students can then practice the transfer of learning.

While the 5E has been proven to be quite effective, the 7E can further help teachers to address the important, essential requirements for learning of eliciting prior understandings and transfer of concepts.

Generative Learning Model

Another model for effective inquiry-based lesson design is the Generative Learning Model (GLM; Osborne & Freyberg, 1985). There are four phases to this model. During the *Preliminary Phase*, the teacher discovers and classifies students' views about a topic. It is then determined what scientific views are necessary. The teacher also must consider the evidence necessary to lead the students to abandon old views. This is accomplished by having students complete surveys or participate in other activities designed to pinpoint their existing understandings.

The second phase is the *Focus Phase*. It is at this point the teacher establishes a context and provides motivating experiences to help students become familiar with materials. Students generally are active in explorations that help them think about what is happening. They generate questions related to the concept at task. Based on prior knowledge and the present experience, students can clarify their own views and share information with the class via discussions and/or displays. The teacher asks open-ended questions to interpret the students' responses and understand changes in students' views.

During the *Challenge Phase*, the teacher facilitates an exchange of views, allowing all interpretations at this time. If necessary, the teacher can encourage further procedures to help present evidence from a scientific viewpoint. Students, in this phase, conduct further testing to check for validity of their views, making comparisons with those of the other pupils in the class and those of the scientific community.

To complete the GLM, students begin the *Application Phase.* The teacher assists students by stimulating and contributing to discussions, and helps students solve advanced problems by directing them to places where they can obtain accurate information. Students are asked to clarify their new views by solving practical problems using the concept learned as a basis. They present solutions to others in the class and suggest further problems that arise from their experiences.

Figure 1.2   5E Lesson Plan—Erosion and Runoff

ENGAGE: Tell the students you are going for a walk outside. Have them discuss and explain what they might see if soil has moved from one place to another. Discuss why this might have happened (suggested responses: erosion, puddles, areas that are on a slant). Take students on a walk outside to make observations of the land. They are to make note of where the soil is worn away or collected in an area. Upon return to the classroom, have students make a list of sites where the soil was worn away or collected. Possible questions: What are the differences between the areas? What do you think caused the differences? Be sure to have students recognize that humans may also be a cause.

EXPLORE: Have students construct a model to investigate how changes may have occurred using suggestions below. Once the model is constructed, have students draw and label a diagram of their model. A prediction should be made about what would happen if it rains. Students should then use the watering can (one cup of water for each landscape model). Observations should be made after water is poured over each area. Wait several minutes and have the students make final observations on the effect of water on their landscape and in the quart jars. Make comparisons with their predictions.

EXPLAIN: Record student results on the board—predictions and final observations. Questions: What actually happened when it rained on your landscapes? What changes took place? What differences did you notice? What happened to the soil? Where did it go and why? Record key statements on the board. Some may include: dirt and water washed away, rain carried soil down the incline, sod held the water better than the other two. Relate students' observations to scientific knowledge. Using student models, have students label erosion and deposition. Students can then define these terms. Students should be aware that soil that has ground cover is less apt to erode and form deposits lower down a hill. Help students understand that water is not the only cause of erosion. It can be caused by wind, people, animals, and so forth. Discuss how crop rotation and how planting in a horizontal fashion will cut down on erosion.

(Continued)

Figure 1.2 (Continued)

EXTENSIONS: Have students use their poorest landscape models and design ways of decreasing or elimination erosion. Students should draw and label a diagram of their planned model and the materials they would use. They will then write a short explanation of why they think their ideas will work to curb erosion. They will need to submit a list of additional materials their models will need. Give students time to build their new landscapes. To enhance this activity with reading and writing, students could research a variety of areas in the country that are the result of erosion: the Grand Canyon, Mississippi River Delta, and so forth. Students could also read selections from *The Grapes of Wrath* by John Steinbeck or *Out of the Dust* by Karen Hesse.

EVALUATION: Take pictures of students' end models and have students do a classroom presentation identifying how and why their models work. As a homework assignment, students could walk around the area where they live looking for areas of erosion and deposition. They could draw, label, and write brief descriptions of their observations.

MATERIALS: Three plastic shoeboxes (cut a hole sized to fit tubing and sealed around the tubing with tape or other adhesive at the bottom of one short side in each container); flexible plastic tubing; quart jars; sod for one container; soil for one container covered with straw; soil for remaining container; watering can with water.

SETUP: Elevate one end of each container. Tubing hanging from each container should be placed in quart jar to collect runoff.

SOURCE: Environmental workshop activity developed by Christine Crane, Rich Gulyas, and Michael Lovegreen.

Figure 1.3 A Generative Learning Model Lesson—Pendulums

PRELIMINARY PHASE: To ascertain students' knowledge.

Begin by telling students a story about a young couple who were taking a stroll through the jungle when they heard a loud noise behind them. When the young man turned to look, he noticed that a herd of elephants was headed in their direction. Both began running to get away from the wild herd. All of a sudden, they came to the edge of a raging river. A quick decision had to be made! They really could not go around the river as it would take too long and there was the possibility of the elephants following. There were two vines hanging down from a tree to help them get to the other side of the river. One vine was shorter than the other. Here is the problem for your group to solve: Which vine should the young man take to get across the pit the quickest? Should he take the short vine or the long vine? Should he take his girlfriend with him or go alone?

Students are encouraged to come up with their own ideas, writing them in their science journals or lab sheets. They must also explain why they made their decisions. The teacher can then ascertain students' views and understanding of pendulums.

FOCUS PHASE: Students should be actively involved in explorations helping them think about the material.

Students are placed in groups selecting materials, collecting data, and placing data in charts in preparation to share with the whole group. Upon completion of their explorations, they will share their conclusions with the whole group.

CHALLENGE PHASE: An exchange of views and interpretations is made at this time. Further procedures may be necessary to present the evidence from a scientific point of view.

Students begin sharing final results. A discussion of pendulums takes place. The group may design a uniform procedure for each group to follow. At this time, the teacher can present a discrepant event with chains and other pendulums to demonstrate change in the center of mass.

APPLICATION PHASE: Advanced problems are given to ascertain students' new understanding of pendulums.

Remind students of times when as children they swung on tree swings. Show them a picture of a swing in a tree. (Two vines hang from the branch of a tree. One side of the branch is higher than the other. The board to sit on is level with the ground.) Explain to the students that unfortunately it swings crooked. In groups, they are to fix the problem by making the board swing straight. They cannot make a tire swing!

SUGGESTED MATERIALS: metric rulers, fishing weights, string, calculators, masking tape, stopwatches

SOURCE: Adapted from Kyle, W., Bonnestetter, R., McCloskey, S., & Fults, B. (1985). What research says: Science through discovery: Students love it. *Science and Children, 23*(2), 39–41.

ASSESSING INQUIRY

Standards-based assessments that specify what students need to know by a specific grade level have become the norm in schools across the country; thus, teachers can match standards to skills that are developed in the curriculum. Assessments can take two basic forms: *traditional assessments* (generally paper-and-pencil tests or quizzes) and *performance/authentic assessments* (require students to demonstrate their knowledge in different formats). For example, in Chapter 4, students' writing projects and, in Chapter 5, students' multimedia projects are ways to demonstrate knowledge. Other examples include:

- **Inquiry-based investigations at the conclusion of a group activity**—The whole group could hand in one report based on group results. A student who disagrees could submit an individual report for separate grading, or the whole group could work together with each student submitting a written report for grading. Finally, the whole group could work together on an investigation with each student keeping his or her own data and submitting individual reports.

- **Teacher observation**—Checklists of students' accomplishments based on instructional objectives make this more manageable.
- **Interviews with students**—This form may be time consuming. Teachers may find it easier to interview a group while they are working on an investigation. Berenson and Carter (1995) suggest that the teacher provide questions and tape student-to-student interviews to review later.
- **Journals**—While there is no specific format, teachers can guide the writing, initially giving focus on what is to be included. These are more fully discussed in Chapter 4.
- **Concept maps**—Students graphically construct relationships of topic. This could be done as a pre-evaluation and then upon completion to show growth of students' understanding. Concept maps may also demonstrate students' misconceptions (Roth, 1992).
- **Drawings**—Drawings done before an activity or lesson can reveal students' initial perceptions and then be compared to final drawings for changes of understanding.
- **Portfolios**—Long-term documentation of students' classroom work is kept in folders or files. Students and teacher have input creating a partnership in the assessment process, and the contents of the portfolio also allow the teacher to assess students' growth. Students can reflect on their work (Paulson & Paulson, 1990). Additionally, portfolios can be vehicles for communication between parents and teacher (Nickelson, 2004).

STANDARDS

When compared with other nations, the United States lags behind in the understanding of science knowledge (Third International Mathematics and Science Study, 1996). Because of federal requirements related to the No Child Left Behind Act, many contemporary reform ideas in science education are reaching practitioners. These ideas are based on advances in cognitive psychology and human development research (Rakow, 1998; Wandersee et al., 1998). The ideas have promoted much debate by those who wish to contest the epistemological basis for learning science present in those reports (Crane, 1998). As a result, the *National Science Education Standards* were developed to provide curriculum and instructional guidelines for quality science education for all students. States have implemented their own standards based on these national standards. Standards describe what students and teachers need to know in order to promote a science-literate society. While some seem intimidated by the standards, most were already being addressed in curriculum before they became formal standards (Rakow, 1998). It is essential that teachers and curriculum coordinators are aware of standards to ensure that standards are met (NRC, 1996).

SUMMARY

Standards are written for teachers to encourage students to become proficient by setting their own personal goals under the guidance of a skilled and knowledgeable teacher. As students mature, their capacity to inquire changes, becoming more sophisticated (Rakow, 1998). Students are more apt to understand the natural world if they are given opportunities to work directly with natural phenomena. They are also more likely to be interested in curriculum if it relates to their own lives. By using their senses to observe and by using scientific instruments, students are capable of extending the power of their senses (National Science Board, 1991) and learn science content more effectively. A student's success is directly related to how the student sees himself or herself as a learner and how the student defines success. Success in science is also determined by how well the curriculum matches the needs of students—developmentally, culturally, and academically (Chamberlain, 2003). Inquiry-based science can be a vehicle to meet the challenges of diversity among students and the need for science literacy in a changing society. The task is not easy, but it is worth the effort.

Whether the 5E or GLM lesson design is used by teachers to frame inquiry lessons in science classrooms, the goals include science literacy and understanding. Throughout this book, the examples provided can be adapted to either model. As you continue reading the following chapters, connections to the proposals of the *National Science Education Standards* (NRC, 1996) may become apparent as we ask you to consider different approaches to teaching science content.

Figure 1.4   Changing Emphases in Science Education

Less emphasis on:

- Memorizing facts and information
- Isolated learning of subject matter disciplines (physical, life, earth science)
- Separating science knowledge and process
- Covering many science topics in a course
- Implementing inquiry as a set of processes
- Activities to demonstrate and verify science content
- One class period investigations
- Emphasis on process skills rather than the overall picture
- Looking for one right answer
- Teacher providing answers
- Doing investigations without defending a conclusion
- Covering a large amount of material allowing for only a few investigations
- Private communication of students' ideas and conclusions to teacher

More emphasis on:

- Understanding science concepts and developing abilities of inquiry
- Integrating all aspects of science content
- Studying a few fundamental science concepts
- Investigative and analytical science questions
- Extended periods of time for investigation
- Allowing for the development or revisions of an explanation
- Communication of students' scientific explanations, ideas, and information
- Allowing more time for investigations in order for students to develop understanding
- Groups of students working together to solve problems
- Coordinating planning, teaching, and assessments

SOURCE: Adapted from National Science Education Standards, NRC, 1996.

2

Textbooks in the Science Classroom

What are your memories of learning to read? What did you choose to read when you were in high school? In what ways have your reading habits changed? What do you think your students read? What might make reading science different from reading other materials? As you read this chapter, reflect upon your answers to these questions and your memories. Think about an experience when you may have had difficulty reading something. Chances are the piece with which you had difficulty was about something with which you had little background experience. When my son and daughter-in-law were dating, he decided to cook her a birthday dinner, found a recipe in a cookbook, then called me in a panic because he didn't know what orange zest was. I talked him through to the spice aisle and tried to convince him that grated orange peel was orange zest. He had little background knowledge, but with guidance, his chicken dish was delicious, or so I hear.

What is reading? It is more than pronouncing words that are printed on a page; reading includes bringing your own understanding to those words. Each word has a dictionary meaning, a *denoted* meaning. However, we bring our own meanings to the words we read, the *connotative* meaning. For instance, the denoted meaning of *dog* might be "a four-legged mammal of the canine species." But you might include in the meaning the memories of your favorite puppy or the big dog that bit you when you were a child. Reading is more than word recognition; it also includes *comprehension*, understanding what we read. There are several factors that contribute to students' understanding of printed materials, including students' abilities and the material itself.

Teachers support their students' quest for knowledge by guiding the learning process and selection of appropriate materials (Llewellyn, 2005). In a secondary science classroom that supports the culture of inquiry, reading can be one of many tools. Due to the nature of inquiry, students identify their goals and purposes for reading whether they develop their own questions or the teacher poses provocative situations. In the following sections, we will look at textbooks and their role in an inquiry-based classroom. Then, we will look at students' abilities to use the material.

QUALITY AND APPROPRIATENESS OF TEXTBOOKS

First, let us consider the quality of the material in textbooks. An extensive report, Project 2061, sponsored by the AAAS, included criteria for the evaluation of textbooks used in middle and high school science. According to the criteria, most textbooks failed miserably at both instructional levels. The AAAS report stated that the textbooks often overemphasized facts and vocabulary, included too many topics, were overloaded with superfluous and confusing graphics and marginal materials, and most shockingly, contained many errors in science content (AAAS, 1993; Roseman, Kesidou, & Stern, 1997). The National Science Teachers Association (NSTA) position, based upon several research studies, suggests that textbooks may include content errors and they do not aid students in understanding the relationships between concepts (Kulm, Roseman, & Treistman, 1999).

Textbooks have also been criticized for not promoting inquiry-based science learning; the "hands-on" activities and lab projects in textbooks are more like recipes and step-by-step procedures, rather than actual investigations based upon student curiosity and questions. Science textbooks, however, can be used as one of many resources in the classroom by teachers who understand the inquiry process and who use their science expertise and their knowledge of students to choose appropriate strategies (Park, 2005).

Science textbooks tend to be written in an impersonal, technical tone with which students often have a hard time connecting to their own experiences. Good readers who have wide experiences are often able to make these connections on their own; however, some students are not able to make the connections. Students may not have the strategies to use textbooks. They may not know how to use such components as their glossaries or indexes. You might suggest that the language arts or English teachers provide this instruction. They probably do. However, students often do not transfer this information. In a departmentalized, compartmentalized educational environment, students do not seem to make the connections.

Recently, while visiting a ninth-grade biology class, I observed students attempting to complete an assignment that required them to read the beginning of a chapter and then answer questions at the end of the assigned section. The students struggled with answering the questions, particularly a question that required them to explain how the uniqueness of a carbon atom made it so versatile. Some of the students stumbled while reading the text and could not explain concepts in their own words. It was clear that the students did not have background understandings of terms such as *chemical bonds, electrons, protons, neutrons, molecules,* and *compounds.* They also had difficulty understanding real-life applications of what they were reading. In the following sections, you will find some suggestions that may have made a difference.

READABILITY OF TEXTS

A factor related to appropriateness of printed material is the *readability* of the material. Is the material appropriate for the grade level and the students for which it is intended? Research suggests that all students, even the best, have difficulty with science textbooks (Crane & Chamberlin, 2004), thus the readability of science textbooks is a major concern.

Organizational structures and supporting formats influence the appropriateness of reading materials. Some characteristics that teachers can examine are as follows: How does the table of contents describe the materials? How do the chapter titles and subheads support an understanding of the organization of the material? How do chapter headings and subheadings aid students in their reading? In what ways are the vocabulary words presented? Are glossaries and indexes easy to use? How do charts and diagrams clarify meanings? Are pages void of pictures or overloaded with graphics? Do pages look disorganized and cluttered? What font and print size are used? In general, look at the usability of the text and consider the appropriateness of the presentation to the developmental needs of the students for whom it is intended.

Why should we be concerned about these aspects of reading in science classes? In secondary content areas, teachers are often more interested in reading to learn than in learning to read. But in reality, content area teachers should have a vested interest in their students' success in reading. Reading is a teaching aid and needs to be used effectively (Roe, Stoodt-Hill, & Burns, 2004). Reading and science are both dynamic processes during which students need to be actively involved to construct knowledge.

Reading in science textbooks necessitates a different approach than students may encounter in traditional reading classes. Typically, students have had more experience reading narratives either in their basal reading texts or in fiction such as the work of Stephen King or the latest romance novels. In inquiry-based classrooms where textbooks are not the main focus of learning, teachers encourage students to look at textbooks as one type of resource. In science class, they will be reading for information. Effective teachers model how to find material related to inquiry problems by using indexes and tables of contents. Teachers model and encourage students to use critical-thinking skills such as questioning authors' assumptions or backgrounds or questioning the accuracy of the information provided. Before assigning material or encouraging students to read specific sections, teachers prepare students for reading by using pre-reading strategies.

Texts may be divided into sections using headings and subheadings. These devices are useful to chunk the material in manageable sections; however, some students may not know how to effectively use these aids. Textbooks may present many concepts in a short selection. Often, each sentence will contain an important concept or bit of information. Furthermore, textbooks introduce specialized or technical information that is science specific. In addition to reading words and sentences in science textbooks, students will be required to read charts, graphs, or diagrams. Effective teachers support students who have difficulty with these tasks.

STUDENTS' READING ABILITIES

Another consideration for the appropriateness of reading materials is students' *reading ability*. Do students have strategies necessary to understand written symbols on the page and are they able to effectively use these strategies? This is an aspect of using textbooks that probably frustrates content area teachers most. Even teachers who are assigned the highest level classes, those with students at the advanced placement level, will have a wide range of reading abilities in a class. There may be very bright students who have reading disabilities and special education services. There may be determined students who are slow readers but remember what they read. There may also be those students who enjoy reading for pleasure but have difficulty reading textbooks. So what do we mean by reading ability?

Reading ability hinges upon a reader's capacity to understand and interpret the printed word. This ability is often measured by scores on standardized tests. These scores provide *estimated* information. We know that a student's ability to read information can vary from subject to subject. Reflect upon your answers for questions in the first paragraph of this chapter. Do you read with the same proficiency in all areas? Additionally, we must also remember that students have different backgrounds that may influence their understanding of material. Idioms can be confusing to those for whom English is not their primary language. Some students may not have experienced situations that would support their understanding. For example, students who have lived on a farm and had experience with cattle breeding may understand Punnet squares while studying genetics more easily than those who have not.

A concept related to reading ability is *fluency*—the speed and accuracy of reading words and phrases. Additionally, fluency includes the ability to read smoothly and expressively. Students may be fluent in their oral language; they may have an impressive command in speech and writing but not be comfortable in reading the work of others. Fluency may be misleading because some students are speed readers and can pronounce words accurately but they do not comprehend what they are reading. On the other hand, some students who are more visual may not be able to use words but can interpret the words on a written page. Fluent readers are able to match their reading rate with the content they are reading. A high correlation has been found between fluency and comprehension. Fluency is especially important because of the amount of reading expected at the secondary levels. This can be especially frustrating for those who must decode words or struggle over vocabulary. Fluency can improve if students have ample opportunities to interact with texts (Roe et al., 2004).

Perhaps it is more productive to consider students' level of ability with the particular material. Generally, we can describe the student interacting with material at the *independent* level, the *instructional* level, or the *frustration* level. Materials at the independent level should have more than 95% fluency and very high comprehension. Comprehension is exhibited when students can explain what they have read in their own words and can ask or answer appropriate questions beyond the literal level. Between 90% and 94% fluency is considered to indicate that material is appropriate for students' instructional level. Typically, older students have a higher fluency during silent reading than they do orally. These levels will be important as lessons and assignments are designed and implemented. Below 90% fluency indicates that the material may be frustrating to the students.

Classroom teachers who need a quick way to assess whether a student is reading at an instructional level can use the old "five-finger test." During oral reading, if the student misses more than 5 words out of 100, the material is probably too hard for the student. Multisyllabic technical terms may not be important for overall fluency. Care must be taken to make sure that students aren't just pronouncing words without understanding them; teachers can ask one or two questions about the passage to check comprehension.

Although standardized test results may be available to suggest comprehension levels, they may not be easily accessible and do take time to interpret. If you have 100 or more students moving through your classroom on a typical day, you may not be able to spend time searching through student files. Informal assessment such as carefully designed discussion questions can provide teachers with an estimate of their students' comprehension. Also, asking students to paraphrase information in the text by writing or diagramming activities may provide insight. Information about relating writing to reading and other activities in a science classroom will be provided in Chapter 4.

MATCHING TEXTS AND STUDENTS

After we have an understanding of our students' reading abilities, we consider material we wish our students to read. There are several readability measures that range from simple to complex that can estimate the appropriateness of material. Most of these measures rely on word counts, sentence lengths, and syllable counts to determine an estimated grade level for the text. A quick Internet search will provide a variety of readability measures such as the Flesch Readability Ease formula, the Fog Index, the Fry Graph, or the Rayor Readability Estimate, many of which have graphs and charts that may be downloaded.

Although readability measures are quick and easy, evaluators must realize that scores are only estimates that may be influenced by several factors. First, if the text includes specialized vocabulary or foreign words, the score may be inaccurate. Furthermore, sentence structure and complexity can have an effect. For instance, long sentences with several clauses and phrases may confuse students by detracting from the main subject and verb. Additionally, because the measures are based on mathematical formulas, influences such as student interests, background knowledge, complexity of ideas, and familiarity with the English language cannot be included in the equations.

Language and literacy abilities—communication, vocabulary, semantic memory, and reading/language arts skills—may be the most important cluster of abilities and skills for achievement. Oral language difficulties are common across categories of exceptionalities. An inability to recall verbal school content or school rules and procedures have been shown to be common characteristics of exceptional students. Students with hearing impairments commonly score several years behind their nondisabled peers in reading and related language arts, and communication disorders commonly occur in students with some types of physical disabilities such as cerebral palsy (Scruggs & Mastropieri, 1993).

Students who have difficulty reading should have more rather than less access to print; this interaction should be more than worksheets and lab reports. However, students with mild disabilities or other special needs may process less print, understand what they read less, and appreciate what they read less. They have to put more effort into understanding words and may not be able to remember large amounts of material at one time. They may also have difficulty making connections among ideas (Mastropieri, Leinart, & Scruggs, 1999). Students with learning disabilities may remember text better if the text is accompanied by visual representations (Scruggs & Mastropieri, 1995).

OTHER CONSIDERATIONS FOR TEXTBOOK EVALUATIONS

Many secondary science teachers use textbooks as a basic staple for learning. The way teachers choose textbooks influences the success of students in their acquisition of knowledge (NSTA, 2005). The challenge is then for science teachers to carefully consider the textbooks they use and to find strategies to effectively use the books.

Many times, we do not have much choice in the textbooks we must use. Some parents believe that students must have a textbook—how else can they learn? If the material is dated or the material is not appropriate for our students' abilities and needs, we must make do. The materials we use in our classrooms may exacerbate differences among our students and hinder their success. Seven forms of bias have been found to be in textbooks (Sadker & Sadker, 2005), but these biases can also be found in other materials. These biases can be applied to many kinds of differences—cultural, gender, ability, or physical. In an inquiry-based classroom where students have learned to pose critical questions, students can also be prompted to critically view the materials. They can help identify biases that may be present and suggest alternative views. Figure 2.1 outlines these biases.

If material is dated, students and teachers together can consult more recent materials and discuss how and why the information has changed. If texts are biased, teachers can encourage students to look at the material critically, to

Figure 2.1   Seven Types of Bias

Linguistic bias—Subtle messages are delivered when language doesn't represent both genders or when it patronizes those with disabilities, those from different cultures, or those of different ages.

Invisibility—When certain groups are underrepresented or neglected within the text, the message suggests that these groups did not make significant contributions to the field.

Stereotyping—Assigning traditional roles or attributes to a particular group may lead to stereotyping.

Imbalance or Selectivity—Topics are left out or treated in an unequal manner. This has recently become a "hot topic" in science fields. In the last few years, the inclusion and treatment of such topics as evolution and cloning in high school curricula has been debated in many states.

Unreality—The material glosses over or avoids controversial issues or portrays contemporary or historical situations unrealistically.

Fragmentation or Isolation—In their attempt to address diversity issues, textbook publishers often put in sidebars or special chapters. In effect, this treatment suggests that a woman (or a black person, or a person with a disability) is unusual and may not normally be a scientist.

Cosmetic—Pictures on the cover or inside suggest a balanced approach, but the text does not support diversity.

SOURCE: Adapted from Sadker, M. P., & Sadker, D. M. (2005). *Teachers, Schools, and Society* (7th ed.). NY: McGraw-Hill.

ask themselves to infer what assumptions the author brings to the material or to verify the information in the text with other materials. Teachers may also choose to provide counterexamples that do not demonstrate bias or choose additional materials that are appropriate. The following sections provide ideas teachers may use to help students achieve content standards and goals using textbooks. These strategies may also be appropriate with other kinds of written materials ranging from journal articles to fiction even though in this chapter we are focusing on textbooks. Alternate forms of reading material will be addressed in Chapter 3. We encourage readers to revisit the concept of inquiry-based science presented in Chapter 1, particularly the Generative Learning Model and the 5E Model explanations. We will point out some examples of how this inquiry pedagogy may use science textbooks.

STRATEGIES FOR USING TEXTBOOK MATERIALS

It is most frustrating to attempt to discuss a reading assignment with students when they clearly haven't read the material. Perhaps you remember having a teacher assign a chapter that you were expected to read for homework and then require you to answer the questions at the end of the chapter. If you were like many high school students, you may have looked at the questions first and then searched the chapter for those answers, ignoring much of the other information in the chapter. Students who are guided through the reading of textbook material are more willing to read the material, comprehend the material better, and participate more in class. If we have a diversified class as suggested in Chapter 1 and want to use textbooks or other reading materials in our inquiry-based classroom, how do we choose what strategies to use?

Some of the challenges for exceptional students in a regular classroom include the expectation for independent study skills and the wide range of subjects that must be mastered concurrently. Additionally, there exists an assumption that students enter classes with an adequate base of content knowledge and skills. Because students who have special needs often work at a slower pace than other students, the pressure to cover a large amount of material in a short time may be overwhelming. Even though students may be able to learn the material, the amount of time allotted may not be sufficient (Mastropieri & Scruggs, 2001).

Modeling strategies increase student achievement. Gaskins and colleagues (Gaskins et al., 1994) completed a yearlong study involving an integrated science and reading curriculum with remedial reading students in a middle school setting. Half of the sample had teachers who modeled additional strategies that the students could use and tell why the strategies would work and how to implement the strategies. All students were given a complex problem to solve. The students who had strategies modeled by the teacher made significant improvement in their ability to state a problem, select materials to solve the problem, and determine a solution for the problem. They were better at demonstrating a conceptual understanding of the later problem.

The state of California published *Essential Elements of Science Instruction for English Learners* in 2004 (Dobb, 2004). This manual suggests that teachers "understand and maintain awareness of the complex political, social, and economic reality" of students for whom English is a second language (p. 11). These students have difficult learning tasks, for not only are they learning science content, but they are also learning vocabulary and nuances of English in often stressful situations. Often they have oral proficiency in social situations with their peers. However, they may not have the reading skills necessary to help them comprehend what they are reading and writing skills to communicate their learning. Dobb also suggests that good teaching strategies that help other students may actually be "instructional life raft[s]" (p. 12) that can save English language learners (ELLs). Even with good academic background preparation in their native languages, these students may need two to three times longer to read science texts, and they may miss major concepts. They have difficulty because the English texts become "moving target[s]" (Cummins, Brown, & Sayers, 2007, p. 51). Inquiry science provides an opportunity for students to practice what they are learning about language while they are learning science concepts as they pose questions, manipulate ideas, work together in groups, and talk about their learning.

Students who are ELLs may also have other cultural differences such as religion and customs. While often this is expected, such differences may also be present among the other students. For instance, a religious or cultural group may not be supportive of afterschool group work or community service projects. Curriculum and materials are often challenged based upon home beliefs. Students who are disadvantaged may have high aspirations or goals but be afraid that they cannot reach their goals (Battistich, Solomon, Kim, Watson, & Schaps, 1995).

Consider the biology scenario presented earlier in this chapter. The material may have been too difficult for students to read and students may not have had adequate background knowledge to comprehend the material. Think about ways you could assess their background knowledge before they read.

PRE-READING ACTIVITIES

According to the 5E Model and the Generative Learning Model, it is important to elicit students' prior knowledge. Before students read a selection in a textbook, they should be guided in the assessment of their own prior knowledge. Good readers are able to do this with little help; however, modeling by the teacher will be confirming to some students' assessment of their own ability, while teacher guidance will help struggling readers develop the strategy. Conduct an activity to engage students so that they can identify what they know and what they need to know. They can generate questions for their inquiry (Huber & Walker, 2002).

Graphic organizers are visual models that can serve many purposes including vocabulary development, advanced organizers, study guides during reading, or review activities. Graphic organizers can take many forms including the ones shown in Figure 2.2. Venn diagrams are excellent for showing similarities and differences. They are helpful when concepts overlap. Pyramids are useful for showing hierarchical relationships. They may also be useful for showing classification systems. Targets are useful for showing central ideas and surrounding issue(s). Circular flow charts can be used to show cyclical arrangements. Lateral flow charts are helpful when showing cause-and-effect relationships. Organizational charts are useful for showing main topics and subtopics.

A quick, well-known graphic organizer is the KWL chart created by Donna Ogle in 1986. Students identify what they already *know* about a subject, form questions to identify what they *would like to learn*, and after reading, they summarize *what they have learned*. This final stage can check their accuracy of prior knowledge as well as summarize their new knowledge. In inquiry-based classrooms, students are encouraged to act like scientists; they consult existing information about their topic. This information may be in a textbook. Note the KWL chart in Figure 2.4. In the first column, the student has shown a misconception about organic and inorganic compounds, stating that organic compounds are "living" or have come from living things. Therefore, the teacher would be sure to include in lessons a discussion of what organic means.

Figure 2.2   Types of Graphic Organizers

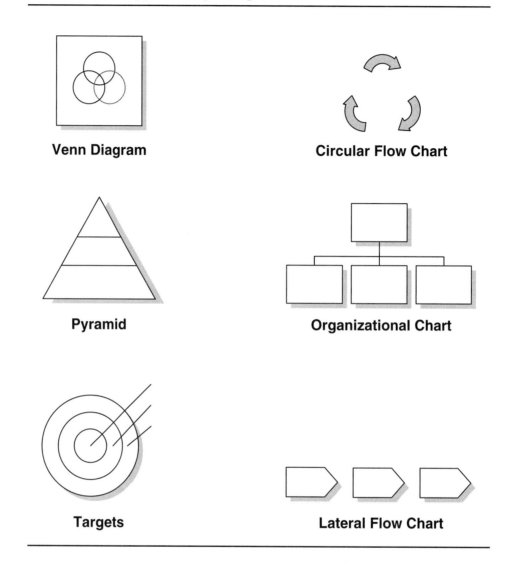

Venn Diagram

Circular Flow Chart

Pyramid

Organizational Chart

Targets

Lateral Flow Chart

Figure 2.3   Steps to Create a Graphic Organizer

1.   Decide how you want to use the organizer.

2.   Identify the concepts that are important.

3.   Consider students' needs and strengths.

4.   Arrange the concepts in a logical manner according to their importance or relationship.

5.   Choose a graphical form that supports or enhances the concept.

Usually the most important concept is at the top or in the center.

Figure 2.4   Sample Entries: A Student-Produced KWL Chart

Organic Compounds and Carbon

What I know . . .	What I want to know . . .	What I have learned . . .
Coal is a carbon.	What is carbonated water?	
All living things are organic compounds.	Is coal an organic compound?	
I heard that carbon has something to do with steroids.		

After determining that a textbook has information that is appropriate and related to a student inquiry, the length of a reading assignment is an initial challenge for the teacher. Consider the concepts addressed, their difficulty, and the manner in which they are presented. Instead of assigning a full chapter, divide the chapter into manageable sections based upon your experience, understanding of content, and knowledge of the students. It may be appropriate to read only specific sections of a chapter.

Some teachers prefer to conduct lab experiences prior to reading assignments rather than the other way around (Llewellyn, 2005). As students work through laboratory activities, they observe situations or reactions, propose hypotheses, and pose questions. Students can classify questions that can be answered by data collection or experimentation or that may need research in written sources. This latter group may include questions related to definition of terms or clarification of concepts leading students to set purposes for inquiry and reading. Because inquiry-based classrooms encourage social interaction to help students construct knowledge, students can pose questions in small groups related to their inquiry. Such activities may be inserted in the Generative Learning Model or the 5E Model formats for science lessons. For instance, in the Preliminary stage of the Generative Learning Model, students are encouraged to seek scientists' views on an issue. During the Challenge stage, students are asked to compare their views to those of the scientists.

Figure 2.5 shows an activity that can be done prior to reading a selection. In this activity, students create a concept web during which they identify issues related to their inquiry and predict the information they may find. The sample shown is a partially completed graphic organizer assuming the students have decided that they needed to find more information about arthropods. They wanted to know the characteristics of arthropods, the different kinds of arthropods, and the habitats of arthropods. Concept webs may be easily constructed by using a word processing program or concept mapping programs such as Inspiration. Details about the program can be found in Chapter 5.

Students may also complete an anticipation guide as shown in Figure 2.6. In this type of activity, students make statements to prove or disprove based upon their reading. In this way, students can verify or challenge their previous understandings of a topic. Key to this step is helping students identify what they already know about a topic and encouraging them to make predictions about what they may learn.

Figure 2.5   Concept Web

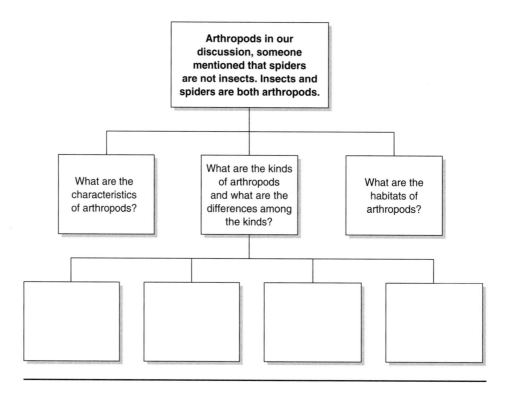

Figure 2.6   Anticipation Guide

Read each statement below. Decide whether you agree or disagree with the statements. After you read the assignment, read the statements again and decide if you agree or disagree. Be able to defend your decisions during our class discussions.

Pre-reading			Post-reading	
Agree	*Disagree*	*Statement*	*Agree*	*Disagree*
		1. When you dissect an arthropod, you will find bones inside their bodies.		
		2. Arthropods live in water or on land.		
		3. Fossils of arthropods can be found in the United States.		

Vocabulary Development

An element of constructivist learning and inquiry-based lessons is communication. Students must be able to communicate their understanding of concepts. A common vocabulary will aid this communication. Although most science textbooks identify vocabulary that will be introduced in a reading selection, preview the material carefully, looking for words that students may find troublesome. Also, look for phrases that may be confusing or troublesome. All of the words in a prescribed vocabulary list may not be important. Eliminate those you believe are not essential in students' understanding of the inquiry problem. In many cases, it is advisable to introduce students to vocabulary prior to their independent reading.

Aspects of vocabulary development include meaningfulness, concreteness, elaboration, and multiple exposures to words (Roe et al., 2004). Because words may have different meanings depending upon context, content-specific applications must be identified. For instance, typically students think of forensics in relationship to criminal investigation or science to solve a problem; the evidence, however, must stand up to public scrutiny. Students who are involved in drama club extracurricular activities may have a different interpretation of forensics—oral performances. Students may enjoy learning that the origin of the word *forensic* is early Latin. The Roman senators had to make arguments supporting ideas in a public forum.

Think back to our biology reading scenario. As the discussion ensued, it appeared that students were having difficulty with the vocabulary words *monomer* and *polymer*. As you look at the following suggestions, think about which ones you might use to help students understand the meanings. Meaningfulness also relates to prior knowledge—do students have experiences with which they can relate the new vocabulary? To engage the concreteness of a vocabulary word, provide a picture or experience that can be connected to the new word. Bring in samples of PVC pipe, Styrofoam cups, quilt batting, or other polymers. When students can associate the word to other words in their vocabularies and understand the word in the new context, the elaboration aspect of vocabulary is engaged. Finally, providing many opportunities for students to see and use the word encourages retention (Roe et al., 2004).

Content-specific vocabulary development has been found to be the most accurate predictor of grades in core content areas such as science (Matkins & Brigham, 1999). Reading fluency can be increased by pre-teaching vocabulary and providing many opportunities for students to use vocabulary. Academic vocabulary can be especially troubling to ELLs and a struggle for those with learning disabilities. Many science-specific words have Greek or Latin roots; structural analysis activities may help not only in science, but also with students' overall proficiency in language (Cummins et al., 2007). Mary Ellsworth (2002) recommends activities such as previewing key vocabulary words and having students create a "word bank" in which they write the definition, use the word in a sentence, draw a picture, and give examples of how the word is used in different situations. She states that these strategies are particularly effective with deaf students who do not have auditory reinforcement. Vocabulary activities, including those that use structural analysis and encourage students to look at word parts, appear to increase the achievement of struggling readers. Other effective strategies include partner retelling, pair/share activities, mnemonics, and graphic organizers (Carnine & Carnine, 2004).

Ellsworth (2002) suggests the use of language experience charts with deaf students, but they can also be effective with other students who have learning difficulties. During a discussion, the teacher writes student responses or comments about an activity on large chart paper. At this time, the teacher can use appropriate science vocabulary. Ellsworth also expands this idea by integrating technology. She suggests that teachers project digital pictures taken during the activity and have the students retell the activity as they view the pictures.

The following are samples of activities that may be used to enhance students' understanding of words necessary for effective communication about topics. Teachers may choose or adapt a strategy based upon their assessment of students' needs. In Figure 2.7, students are asked to identify parts of words (structural analysis). By analyzing root words, prefixes, and suffixes, students can not only learn the words directly connected to their study, but they can also learn skills that they may apply to independent reading. Pages you can copy to aid in structural analysis can be found at the end of this chapter. In Figure 2.8, students are asked to make connections among words that have similar origins and see how these words connect to a theme.

Figure 2.7   Structural Analysis

Structural analysis aids the understanding of words by considering the meanings of parts of words. Typically, we look at prefixes, suffixes, and root words. You may be interested in the etymology, or historical background, of words. Each field of science has vocabulary particularly related to the field. When you learn some of the common root words, you may be able to decode new words when you encounter them.

Example 1:
>   Bio – related to living things
>   Luminescence – related to light
>   Bioluminescence – production of light by living things such as fireflies

Example 2:
>   Arthro – joint
>   Pod – foot or leg
>   Arthropods – animals that have segmented bodies and pairs of legs

Directions: Use the handouts provided to predict the meanings of these words:

Endoplasmic _____

Anticoagulant _____

Keep the handouts in your notebooks so you can use them as you encounter more vocabulary words that stump you.

Figure 2.8   Vocabulary Web

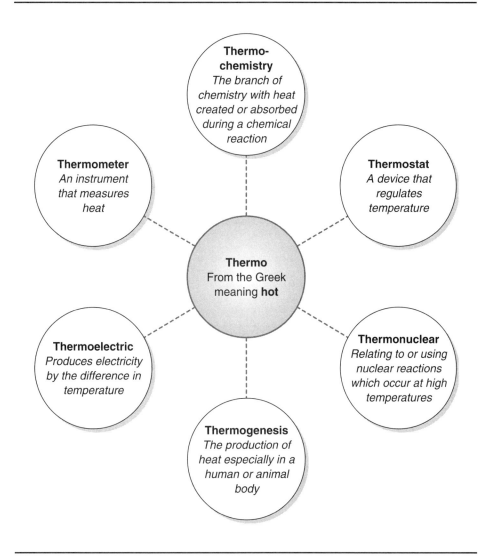

In the Word Box Activity (Figure 2.9), information requested can be adjusted to suit the needs of students and the curriculum. This activity encourages students to use higher-order thinking when they create an analogy, simile, or metaphor. Students stretch their creativity as they do so. At first, students may have difficulty with analogies, similes, or metaphors because they require higher-order thinking skills such as analysis and synthesis. To help students, have an analogy, simile, or metaphor to complete on the board when students enter the room; discuss possibilities and why those possibilities would be appropriate. For example, put on the board "A polymer is like a _____." Perhaps an answer could be a quilt. The rationale may be explained: "A quilt is made up of several blocks sewn together to make a design. Polymers are made up of monomers to make a bigger polymer." Presenting students with a line from a poem that uses simile or metaphor can provoke creative discussions. At the end of this chapter, we have included some other vocabulary resources you may wish to use.

Figure 2.9   Word Box Activity

Vocabulary Word:	
Definition in my own words	Analogy, simile, or metaphor
Word used in a sentence	Picture or diagram

Figure 2.10   Tips for Vocabulary Development

1. Use vocabulary words as much as possible. Repetition helps.

2. Link word study to content; do not study words in isolation.

3. Guide students through content so meanings can be supported by the context of the sentence or paragraph.

4. Encourage students to make connections to other words; synonyms, antonyms, analogies.

5. Help students identify parts of words that have meanings.

6. Limit the number of new vocabulary words. Choose the most important words from lists that may be provided in the textbook.

7. Use your experience to identify words that may be troublesome to students. These words *may not* be on textbook lists.

8. Provide visual and auditory experiences with vocabulary for students.

9. Use bulletin boards or "word walls" to display frequently used technical or unit-related vocabulary.

10. Play with words. Students like to have fun.

Setting a Purpose for Reading

Clearly identify a *purpose for reading*. The Focus stage of the Generative Learning Model suggests that teachers provide motivating experiences. Often, students are more motivated if they develop their own questions for the reading. At the beginning of a unit of inquiry, students could engage in a variation of 20 Questions. Instead of answering 20 questions, they could ask them. Make a large chart of questions students would like to have answered during the study. Put the questions in the language that students use and in the order the questions are asked. Remind students that there are no "stupid" questions. As the answers are found during the investigations, check the question off the list. Students will often attempt to answer some questions on their own; they may do research outside of class and actually compete to find answers. Typically, many questions will be ones that the teacher will include in the curriculum anyway; there may also be some questions that will stump the teacher. When the teacher models research and inquiry (and admits he or she doesn't know everything), a positive atmosphere can result (see Figure 2.11). Another way to encourage students to identify questions for inquiry is to use the KWL chart discussed previously and list their questions under the W column.

Before students begin reading themselves, read some sections aloud and model thought processes that you use when you are reading. For instance, when you come to an interesting concept that can be connected to a real-life application, stop and "think aloud" about the connection. Or when you come to a difficult word, stop and analyze the parts of the word or discuss the origin of the word. By modeling effective reading strategies, you will provide students with tools they may use during reading (Huber & Walker, 2002). For instance, say, "I see the phrase, *intermolecular forces*. Hmmm, I know that *inter* means *between*, so the forces must be between molecules. Oh yes, I remember in class we talked about how molecules can attract each other."

Figure 2.11   Twenty Questions About Polymers

1.   How do monomers combine to be polymers?

2.   Are there different kinds of monomers?

3.   What are some other kinds of polymers that we see every day?

4.   Are all polymers combined chemically in the same way?

5.   Are all polymers the same-sized molecules?

6.   If plastic is a polymer, is glass a polymer?

7.   Are all polymers organic?

8.   Do polymers "act" differently than monomers?

9.   How can we make some polymers?

10.   How do we know how polymers work?

11.   Do any of the factories around here make polymers?

12.   Could polymers be poisonous?

13.   How are polymers named?

14.   Who invented polymers?

15.   Are there different complexities of polymers?

16.   Can polymers be combined to make larger polymers?

17.   What kind of college education would I need to invent polymers?

18.   Are polymers found in nature?

19.   Does heat or cold change polymers?

20.   Can we make some polymers in class?

ACTIVITIES DURING READING

After pre-reading activities have piqued students' interest, a goal is to have students be active in the reading process. To encourage this, it may be appropriate to provide students with some tasks to do while they read. Tasks may be guides developed by the teacher, a list of questions to which students must compose a written response, or something that students must be prepared to do after they have completed the reading. Tasks chosen vary according to the difficulty of the material, the motivation students have for reading the material, or students' abilities to read without assistance.

Guides may be customized to suit the inquiry students have identified. They may require students to paraphrase content ideas in writing, or they may include graphic organizers such as flow charts or other graphic representations. Guides should encourage more than rote learning and should require students to do more than copy answers from the book. Students should be encouraged to use higher-order thinking during which they will be able to interpret what they read into their own words and apply new knowledge. Students should also have an opportunity to analyze ideas, synthesize ideas to create new products, and evaluate ideas critically.

A feature analysis chart is graphic organizer that can help students visualize relationships between concepts (Roe, Stoodt-Hill, & Burns, 2007). In Figure 2.12, students are comparing and contrasting characteristics of lampreys, sharks, and perch. Students can complete the chart while reading an assignment or while making observations. Students are asked to indicate whether the fish exhibit the characteristic listed at the top of the column. After the chart is completed, students can be prompted to make inferences about the fish and use the chart as a basis for classroom discussions or writing.

Figure 2.12   Feature Analysis Chart

While you are reading, look for characteristics of these fish. In the columns next to each of the fish, answer the questions at the top of the columns.

Kind of fish	*Jaws? Yes or No*	*Scales? Yes or No*	*Skeleton? Cartilage or Bone*	*Kind of food?*	*Number of fins?*
Lamprey	No	No	Cartilage	Decaying tissue or parasites	No fins
Shark	Yes	Yes	Cartilage	Carnivore	
Perch			Bones		

When teachers provide students with a written guide for assigned readings, students will be given support. These written guides may also be used as support after reading. McKenna and Robinson (2006) suggest that the belief that only poorer students need written guides is false. They suggest that guides

Figure 2.13   Reasons for Using Reading Guides

- Guides help students focus attention on what is important.
- Reading is made active, physical, when students must write along with reading.
- Students must translate what they are reading to answer questions on the guide.
- Writing enables students to organize, extend, and refine what they have read.
- Guides can be used for review or to clarify terms needed for upcoming activities.
- Guides can help students communicate ideas in discussion.
- Guides that are used effectively increase comprehension.

SOURCE: Adapted from McKenna, M. C., & Robinson, R. D. (2006). *Teaching through Text: Reading and Writing in the Content Areas* (4th ed.). Boston: Pearson Education, Inc.

support better students by increasing comprehension. They also debunk the idea that reading guides should only be provided for difficult reading passages. Guides can be designed to focus students on key points that directly relate to questions they posed. Because science reading has unique demands upon students, they may have difficulty focusing on key ideas. We want students to be actively engaged with material and to have a dialogue with written words. Students who stop to paraphrase an author's words or ask questions are being active. Successful students are able to monitor their own understandings and identify ideas that need clarification.

Figure 2.14   Suggestions for Designing Reading Guides

- Consider the reading ability of the students. Those who may need more support may require different kinds of guides than those who are more independent readers. Some readers may benefit from graphic organizers, while others may be more comfortable with guides that require more paraphrasing and writing.
- Consider the purpose for the reading. Focus on questions directly related to the inquiry.
- Avoid making the guide text heavy. Do not make the guide more difficult or cumbersome to complete than the reading.
- Ask students to use different levels of thinking: literal, inferential, and critical.

SOURCE: Adapted from McKenna, M. C., & Robinson, R. D. (2006). *Teaching through Text: Reading and Writing in the Content Areas* (4th ed.). Boston: Pearson Education, Inc.

Students may benefit from reaction guides such as the one presented in Figure 2.15. In this activity, students are making personal connections, identifying ideas they believe are important, and questioning what they read or how the reading can apply to their inquiry.

Figure 2.15   Reaction Guide

Reading selection		
Something that surprised me was . . . **!**	I can relate to . . . ~	I don't understand . . . **?**
What I think is important is . . . *	Words or ideas that were new to me #	Another comment **&**

SOURCE: Adapted from an activity used by Dr. Rachael Hungerford, Lycoming College, Williamsport, PA. Used with permission.

Read, Reflect, and Question is an activity that encourages students to be critical readers. This activity may be done in their notebooks or on note cards. The teacher may collect the activity to assess students' understanding of the material, or the activity can be used to guide group discussions. Figure 2.16 outlines the procedures for this activity.

Figure 2.16   Read, Reflect, and Question

Write the reading selection pages at the top of your page or note card.

List 5–10 important ideas or pieces of information you learned from your reading.

Write 1–2 paragraphs during which you answer these questions: How did this relate to what you already knew about the topic? Did it agree or disagree with your previous knowledge? Do you have any personal connections to the information?

List 3–5 questions about the information. You may question the author's accuracy or point of view. You may also ask questions to clarify something that you did not understand or that you think would be good for group discussion.

SOURCE: Adapted from an activity used by Dr. Rachael Hungerford, Lycoming College, Williamsport, PA. Used with permission.

Another useful strategy during reading is effective note taking. We cannot assume that all students know how to take notes while reading, nor can we assume that one method of note taking is useful for all students. A highly recommended note-taking system is the Cornell system, which suggests that students divide their note paper into two columns. In the left column, students write key words or ideas; in the right column, students provide details or support. This may be useful to some students; however, other students may need a more visual representation of ideas. Therefore, it is important to help students understand the role of note taking and to develop a system that works for each individual. When teachers model or use several different methods that support different learning styles and needs, students have a repertoire from which to choose.

It may be appropriate to have each person in a group read a different selection of an assigned reading. This could be a variation of a jigsaw activity. Jigsaw activities were developed in the 1970s by Elliot Aronson (Social Psychology Network, 2006). Each student takes notes on his or her own section and then explains the information to the rest of the group. Students could use reading guides that were provided or take their own notes. If more than one group is doing the same set of readings, set aside a time when all students who read the same section can meet to discuss what they learned. Students then go back to their own groups and discuss their sections. Remind students that each person is ultimately responsible for all the information in the entire article. This activity supports the concept of social construction of knowledge, which is important in the constructivist perspective. Additionally, it allows students to communicate their understandings of science concepts. Think back to the concept web presented in Figure 2.5. The students were studying arthropods. Suppose the textbook had sections titled *Spiders, Crustaceans, Insects, and Other Arthropods*. Assign each section to a student member of a group. Students would be responsible for gathering information from their section and then sharing the information with their group and ultimately with the whole class. The whole class could then participate in activities that addressed similarities and differences between the kinds of arthropods.

Whatever strategy teachers choose to support their students while reading, essentially, the purpose is to help students read informational material. Activities that can serve many purposes can use time efficiently. For example, a reading strategy that is used as part of a discussion, used to clarify issues raised during a lab activity, and used when students are communicating results can provide continuity and use time effectively.

POST-READING ACTIVITIES

Post-reading activities serve several purposes. They can be used by teachers to assess students' understanding of text material. After reading, opportunities for students to analyze ideas, synthesize ideas, to create new products, and to critically evaluate ideas consolidate student learning from reading assignments. There are many strategies that teachers can employ that fit into the 5E Model or Generative Learning Model. Students use content knowledge to compare their understandings to scientifically accepted explanations of concepts.

Discussions encourage students to develop understanding of content and identify areas of inadequacies of content knowledge. Discussions, however, may actually be mere recitation of facts unless teachers design discussions to encourage student involvement (McKenna & Robinson, 2006). Classroom atmospheres in which students are willing to take risks and share ideas and opinions facilitate effective post-reading strategies. Student-generated questions as suggested in the Read, Reflect, and Question activity can be a start to further investigation or a refinement of an inquiry. Anticipation guides can also be used to help students clarify their own understanding of the material.

Adolescents like to have fun and many enjoy challenging word or code puzzles. Teachers often use puzzles for times when there are a few extra minutes at the end of a period or when some students finish labs before others. They are also useful fillers for folders that we leave for substitute teachers. Figure 2.17 shows a cryptogram that is a particularly challenging type of puzzle. This activity reinforces a low-level understanding but challenges students to solve a puzzle. Students' thinking can be encouraged by starting with literal questions, then asking students to make inferences based upon their answers, and finally encouraging students to ask critical, evaluative questions about inferences that were made.

Figure 2.17 Cryptogram

After your reading, solve this cryptogram.

Q   EXQK   DQCCTI   DQO   Q   SITQP   QRJQVPST   WTEQHOT

–   ————   ——————   ———   –   —————   ————————   ———————

PDT   AHXEIHC   FO   EXBOT   PB   PDC   VQFX

———   ———————   ——   —————   ——   ———   ————

A = F   M = Z   Y = P

B = O   N = Y   Z = K

C = M   O = S

D = H   P = T

E = C   Q = A   Ms. Johnson Says:

F = I   R = D

G = J   S = G   HINT: Solving
this cryptogram
will be easier if you
remember the
principles of a lever.

H = U   T = E

I = R   U = Q

J = V   V = N

K = W   W = B

L = X   X = L

Find the clue letter in the cryptogram in the list on the left. Find the letter in the right column that corresponds with the letter in the clue. Write the letter from the right column in the blank above the clue letter. The letters should spell out a message.

Example: The first clue is Q; so we write an A in the blank above the Q.

The answer to the cryptogram is: A claw hammer has a great mechanical advantage because the fulcrum is close to the nail. As long as this sentence was not taken directly from the reading but requires students to apply a concept, this is not the lowest level of thinking but is more consistent with the comprehension level in Bloom's taxonomy, which requires students to be able to paraphrase rather than give definitions. Students may also see how a scientific concept is applied to a new situation.

To design a cryptogram, make two columns on a sheet of paper. Write down the letters of the alphabet in the left column. Next to this column, write another alphabet, but this time mix the order of the letters. Put equal signs between the letters of the two columns. Write a sentence containing information that you want students to remember from their reading. For each letter in your sentence, substitute the letter in the right column for each letter in the left column. Encourage students to make their own cryptograms that you can use for a class review. Figure 2.18 gives hints for solving a cryptogram. The hints suggest to students that they can use statistics to solve the puzzle.

Figure 2.18   Hints for Solving a Cryptogram

- The vowels of the English language comprise about 40% of the letters of words.
- L, N, R, S, and T comprise about 30% of letters in English words.
- J, K, Q, X, and Z comprise about 2% of letters in English words.
- The letter E appears most frequently and "THE" is the most common English word.
- Count the number of times each letter appears in the cryptogram.
- Try to match the cryptogram letters with the real alphabet letters based upon these percentages.

Writing while they are reading and after they finish reading encourages students to interpret what they have learned. Writing as a form of communication enhances student learning. Writing after reading fits well within the 5E Model as students explain their understandings. They can elaborate by applying their understandings to new situations by creating literary works on their own. Writing in science will be explored in more detail in Chapter 4.

Higher-order thinking activities in the 5E Model and Generative Learning Model can provide information to assess student comprehension either by the teacher or by students themselves. Instead of questions at the end of the chapter, quizzes, or tests, authentic or performance activities can show what students know (Winebrenner, 1996). This fits into the Evaluation portion of the 5E Model and the Application stage of the Generative Learning Model.

Essentially, the activities encourage students to consider how reading addressed questions raised in their inquiry. In inquiry-based science, the process of learning science does not stop with reading or hands-on activities in textbooks. Information is applied and related to other knowledge. Facts are not learned in isolation but connected to real-life situations or compared to information found in other reading material.

SUMMARY

In this chapter, we discussed the use of textbooks in an inquiry-based classroom. We pointed out that textbooks are not the primary instructional tool in the classroom. We also presented ideas for vocabulary development and pre-reading, during reading, and post-reading strategies that may be applied to reading many types of material. Additionally, some criteria for evaluating textbooks may be applied to other material. On the following pages, you will find structural analysis materials that you may copy to use with your textbook. The next chapter continues the discussion of reading outside the textbook.

Figure 2.19   Using Textbooks in an Inquiry-Based Science Classroom

- Choose selections carefully. It is not necessary to read the whole book or even the whole chapter. The selection should be chosen to meet the needs of the inquiry.
- Evaluate the selection for accurate content and appropriateness to student needs.
- Match the reading selection to students' abilities.
- Prepare students for reading the material. Preview challenging vocabulary. Help students frame a purpose for reading.
- Provide support for students while they are reading. Some students may need more support than others. Support may be in the form of guides or note-taking skills.
- Do something with the material after it is read. Make sure students evaluate the material for content and application to their inquiry. Connect information to real-life situations or other reading materials.

Common Greek Roots of Words

In science, many of our vocabulary words have Greek roots. Below are some of the common ones. Keep this sheet in your science notebook and add your own words as you encounter them.

Greek Root	Meaning	Words You May See
Auto	Self	Automatic
Derm	Skin	Dermatitis, hypodermic
Haem or hem	Blood	Hemoglobin
Hydra (hydro)	Water	Hydroelectric
Hyper	Above	Hyperthermia
Hypo	Below, too little, beneath	Hypodermic
Lith	Stone	Lithology
Meter	Measure	Thermometer
Therm	Heat	Thermometer, hyperthermia
Tope (topos)	Place	Topographical map

Common Latin Roots of Words

In science, many of our vocabulary words have Latin roots. Below are some of the common ones. Keep this sheet in your science notebook and add your own words as you encounter them.

Latin Root	Meaning	Words You May See
Aud	Hear	Audio
Carbon	Carbon – coal	Carboniferous
Chron	Time	Chronological
Cred	Trust or believe	Credible
Duct (ducere)	Lead	Conduct
Gen	Race, family	Genetics
Gram	Written	Diagram
Ject	Throw	Eject
Log	Word	Dialogue
Man	Hand	Manual
Phon	Sound	Telephone
Port	Carry	Transport
Spec	See	Spectacle, inspect
Tempor	Time	Temporary
Tract	Pull	Contract
Voc	Voice	Vocal

Common Prefixes

In science, many of our vocabulary words contain prefixes. Below are some of the common ones. Keep this sheet in your science notebook and add your own words as you encounter them.

Prefix	Meaning	Words You May See
Anti-	Against	Anticoagulant
Counter-	Opposite	Counteract
De-	Make the opposite of	Decipher
Dis-	Not, opposite	Disengage
Hyper-	More than normal	Hypersensitive
Il-	Not	Illogical
Im- or in-	Not	Inactive
Mal-	Bad	Maladapted
Mis-	Wrong, not	Misaligned
Mono-	One	Monocellular
Sub-	Under, below	Subzero, submarine, subsoil
Super-	Above, beyond	Supernova, supersonic

Common Suffixes

In science, many of our vocabulary words use suffixes. Below are some of the common ones. Keep this sheet in your science notebook and add your own words as you encounter them.

Suffix	Meaning	Words You May See
-able	Capable	Malleable
-ation	Action or process	Chlorination
-ic	Having the nature of	Sulfuric
-ite	Native, product, rock, adherent, follower of	Suburbanite, metabolite, satellite
-ize	Cause to conform or resemble	Oxidize
-ous	Having the qualities of	Odorous

3

Beyond the Textbook

Write the alphabet A to Z in a column. Next to each letter write the name of something you read. Think out of the box. Respondents to this task often propose answers such as "yellow pages" for Y or "train schedules" for T. Some of the letters will be difficult, and you may think your answer is wacky. That's okay. If you have a chance, ask a colleague to do a similar activity. Compare your answers. In real-life situations, we read more than we are aware. Take time to look around your science classroom. What reading is available beyond the textbook? Are there posters, magazines, graphs, or charts? Did you bring in the daily newspaper? If so, you have a good start for creating a literature-rich classroom to support inquiry. When you hear the word *literature* you may think of literature courses in high school where you studied novels, plays, or poetry. You may have positive or negative feelings about those experiences. We will expand the definition of literature and will consider other reading materials.

Why should we use different kinds of reading materials in science class? Newspapers, magazines, and research reports may be more current than what is available in textbooks. Material can be chosen to match different reading levels and learning styles of diverse students. The materials may provide different perspectives and encourage abstract thinking. Students may be able to connect science content to everyday life, a goal for good science teaching. Combinations of nonfiction, fiction, and poetry can serve to ground science instruction and keep motivation high. Fiction is an excellent resource to follow up on lessons and further develop language and content connections. Poetry can set the stage for a science lesson and provide a brief but powerful anticipatory setting for the introduction of new science concepts (Hadaway, Vardell, & Young, 2002).

Reading outside the textbook can be a valuable tool when students are engaged in topics related to science, technology, and society (STS). Stories found in literature selections can pose questions about how science has or may have influenced society or history. For instance, *The House of the Scorpion* by Nancy Farmer (2002) is a novel for adolescents addressing the issue of cloning, especially how cloning may influence an individual. An informational book that could be used in conjunction with Farmer's book is *Exploring Science and Medical Discoveries—Cloning*, edited by Nancy Harris (2004), which tells the story of the cloned sheep Dolly, the history of cloning, and controversies about cloning. Lois Lowry's book, *The Giver* (1993) also provides a provocative look at a futuristic society and can be used when teaching about genetic manipulation, science ethics, and end-of-life issues.

Skills in science are similar to those used in reading. In science, students use their senses to gather information; in reading, seeing, hearing, and listening are used. In science, we predict and validate: in reading, students do the same. In science, we collect data; in reading, students take notes, use different parts of books, record, and organize information. In science, we investigate; in reading, students ask questions, look for relationships, and follow procedures. In science, we interpret data; in reading, students recognize cause-and-effect relationships, organize facts, summarize, and think inductively and deductively. In science, we classify; in reading, students compare and contrast, arrange, and sequence ideas. In science, we form conclusions; in reading, students generalize, analyze, identify main ideas, establish relationships, and use information. In science, we communicate results; in reading, students describe clearly (Butzow & Butzow, 2000).

If your students are reading materials other than textbooks as part of their research, pre-reading, during reading, and post-reading activities are still important. Students identify their purpose for reading, they understand crucial vocabulary, and they summarize or evaluate the information. For this reason, the strategies from the textbook chapter will not be discussed here in depth. Instead, we will look at types of materials, their uses, and particular challenges that may arise when using the material.

Trade books, a term that refers to books that are typically available to the general public in bookstores and libraries, can increase students' interest in science while improving reading skills. Science can be viewed from a different and real-to-life perspective with the use of trade books in place of textbooks (Stiffler, 1992). With the need for individualization to meet the needs of students' reading differences, this has proven to be beneficial because for some students, abstract concepts are more easily explained (Wiley & Royce, 1999).

If we consider the steps in science lesson design, nontextbook reading materials can be easily included. For instance, a selection can be presented prior to beginning a unit to arouse curiosity in a topic. Did you ever consider why different kinds of cookies are better "dunkers" than others or why the milk moves up the cookie when the cookie is dunked? A useful book, *How to Dunk a Doughnut* by Len Fisher (2002) is a great conversation starter. A short reading from this book would be a good introduction to the concept of capillary action and could provoke substantial scientific inquiry questions. Applications to other areas of science are also included in the fascinating book. Several other such books are listed at the end of this chapter.

LITERATURE FOR ADOLESCENTS

Literature specifically targeting adolescents is basically a 20th-century phenomenon. In earlier history, books and stories for children and adolescents were not considered "literature" and were not highly regarded. In the 1700s, material for young adults was often based upon Puritan or religious influences and was very didactic. In the last half of the 19th century, however, adventure novels became popularized by such works as *Ivanhoe* by Sir Walter Scott, *Robinson Crusoe* by Robert Louis Stevenson, and *Tom Sawyer* by Mark Twain. At the beginning of the 20th century, popular books included *Peter Pan*, *The Wizard of Oz*, and *Wind in the Willows.*

Later, Horatio Alger wrote a series of books for boys and developed a prototype character, Ragged Dick, who embodied the American dream—he pulled himself up by his bootstraps and became successful. Thus the saying that someone's life was a "Horatio Alger story" was born. Edward Stratemeyer, a clever publisher, promoted series books including the Rover Boys, the Bobbsey Twins, the Hardy Boys, and Nancy Drew mysteries. Stratemeyer's name is little known; the books in the series were written by contract writers after a general plot outline was given to them. It comes as a shock to many when they learn that Carolyn Keene (fictional name for Nancy Drew authors) never existed.

In the 1950s, adolescent and young adult literature focused on traditional social behavior—family, jobs, athletics, and so forth. Most focused on acceptable, middle-class situations. Pregnancy, alcoholism, and divorce were used to give examples of unacceptable behaviors. In the late 1960s, realistic fiction became popular. Situations in novels began to mirror situations that were more consistent with adolescent experiences. Groundbreaking books were *The Outsiders* by S. E. Hinton (1967) and *The Pigman* by Paul Zindel (1968). The 1970s yielded a controversial young adult book, *The Chocolate War*, by Robert Cormier (1974); the 1980s and 1990s brought even more books that captured the interest of young people. Adolescents also became fascinated with science fiction and fantasy.

Overall, adolescent literature typically has characteristics that set it apart from literature designed for other ages. Adolescent books are usually written from the viewpoint of young people. Parents don't have a major role in the story unless they are the cause of conflict. The adolescent characters usually relate better to the elderly—grandparents or an elderly neighbor, for example—or other adults such as teachers. The literature is typically fast paced and deals with emotions that are important to adolescents. In general, the books are optimistic and the characters make worthy accomplishments (Nilsen & Donelson, 2001).

Today, adolescent and young adult literature is big business. J. K. Rowling has become a billionaire from creating Harry Potter! Teachers can tap into this phenomenon by using the book *The Science of Harry Potter* (Highfield, 2002). The number of books published each year is astonishing and the quality of books varies. It is beyond the scope of this book to go into a more detailed history of adolescent/young adult books. However, there are many resources available for those who wish to delve into the topic. One such text is *Children's*

Literature, edited by Wendy Mass (2001), which includes articles that discuss the evolution and trends of literature for children and adolescents. Refer to the 5E Model in Chapter 1. Note how the books *The Grapes of Wrath* by John Steinbeck and *Out of the Dust* by Karen Hesse were integrated.

Some suggest that reading a variety of materials, including fiction, makes students better readers, especially those who have learning difficulties (Downing, 2005). Do adolescents read fiction because they are better readers or are they better readers because they read fiction? We won't get into the correlation or causation debate. We do know that content area teachers are being encouraged to incorporate outside readings into their classes. There are many content area reading textbooks that provide more details and ideas for using literature in science. One text, *Content Area Reading: Literacy and Learning Across the Curriculum* by R. T. Vacca and J. L. Vacca (2005), presents an in-depth discussion of using trade books that range from picture books to young adult literature. *Integrating Literature in the Content Areas: Enhancing Adolescent Learning and Literacy* (Kane, 2007) has over 100 annotations of science-related books representing five genres and strategies for using them.

GENRES OF TRADE BOOKS

Books that we read can be divided into two basic categories: fiction and nonfiction. Nonfiction materials in this category include biographies, autobiographies, memoirs, atlases, content-specific books, and even cookbooks. Fiction materials can be subdivided into two groups: realistic and nonrealistic. Realistic fiction can possibly happen while nonrealistic cannot. We will spend most of the chapter on fiction, but will touch on nonfiction. At the end of the chapter, we include an annotated bibliography of selected books to get you started in your search for books you might want to use. However, we find visiting a bookstore, one with comfortable chairs and reading areas, is a great way to start your personal collection. You may want to begin your collection with topics that are close to you—your environment or your hobbies. If you live near the ocean, look for books about marine life, ship building, or tides. If you like to ski, look for books about snow-covered mountains, avalanches, weather, or ski equipment. Think about the muscles you use to swim or ski, the physics that go into building a ship, or skiing down a mountain. Invest yourself in your collection!

Some types of literature that teachers may find applicable to science classes include but are certainly not limited to:

- **Science fiction**—According to Applewhite Minyard (1998), "Science fiction is, in a sense, an oxymoron" (p. xi). Events and ideas are based on scientific facts or principles and the stories employ characteristics of fiction. The stories may center on future situations that may flow from the science or possibilities of how our world could be different. Mary Shelley's *Frankenstein,* written in 1818, is considered by many to be the beginning of the genre. Well-known novels such as Jules Verne's *Journey to the Center of the Earth* and H. G. Wells's *The Time Machine* and *War of* *the Worlds* are classics. Michael Crichton's *Jurassic Park* (1991) is a contemporary example that could be used in a biology class.

According to Zigo and Moore (2004), high school English teachers often do not include science fiction in their curricula. Critics suggest the genre isn't quality literature; however, it is becoming more accepted in the academic arena. Among the hundreds of titles published, some are excellent resources for the classroom (Minyard, 1998). Zigo and Moore also suggest that reading science fiction actually takes more sophistication and skill than most believe. Vocabulary development and the ability to use contextual clues are enhanced during reading. Students can read older science fiction and compare the scientific speculation by the author to what is known in contemporary science.

Minyard's (1998) book, *Decades of Science Fiction*, is an excellent resource for any science or literature teacher who may be contemplating the inclusion of science fiction in the curriculum. The author provides historical contexts for science fiction written from prior to World War I to the 1990s. He suggests that knowing the history of an era helps readers understand the stories and appreciate science developments in this context. Chapters include time lines of history, discussions of authors and their works, and for some decades, science fiction in other media. Minyard includes short stories that may be used along with suggestions for writing assignments. Instructors are cautioned to evaluate the materials for appropriateness for young readers. Another valuable resource is *Teaching Science Fact with Science Fiction* by Gary Raham (2004).

- **Fantasy**—Many of the scenarios or activities in fantasy books can't happen in the world as we know it; the stories are somewhat real, but the reader may need to suspend belief in some areas. High fantasy includes the theme of the struggle between good and evil such as *Lord of the Rings* by J. R. R. Tolkien or *A Wrinkle in Time* by Madeleine L'Engle. L'Engle's fascination with quantum physics shows in *A Wrinkle in Time*, the first in a series that dealt with time. Jane Yolen, a contemporary author and a past president of the Science Fiction Writers of America, wrote fantasy novels for adolescents and adults that often ask readers to contemplate conditions of modern life. For example, her Pit Dragon trilogy books ask readers to consider the value of all life forms and how life forms depend upon each other.

- **Mystery**—Science is about solving mysteries about our world and beyond. Sherlock Holmes's crime-solving expertise provides mystery-solving examples that can easily be incorporated in the science classroom. Chemistry flows through his mysteries as does the importance of observation and systematic analysis. You may want to find the book *The Science of Sherlock Holmes* (Wagner, 2006). Students who are attracted by TV forensic crime scene investigation may be interested in *The Forensic Casebook: The Science of Crime Scene Investigation* (Genge, 2002). Students may also enjoy reading about how scientists solve mysteries of diseases such as in Richard Preston's *The Hot Zone* (1994), which is discussed later in this chapter.

- **Horror**—Some teens gravitate toward horror stories, but horror stories are difficult to define. Horror is not really a genre but is an emotional reaction to reading. What may constitute horror to one person may not be horrific to another. Supernatural elements are not necessary to horror—if the reading gives you a sickening feeling, it can be horrifying. For instance, *Phineas Gage: A Gruesome but True Story of Brain Science* by John Fleischman (2002) may be horrifying to one reader and fascinating to another. Other works that often fall into the category of horror include Bram Stoker's *Dracula*, Mary Shelley's *Frankenstein*, and Edgar Allan Poe's and Stephen King's works. An excellent anthology that teachers and students could use to find science connection in horror books is *Presenting Young Adult Horror* by Cosette Kies (1992).

- **Biographies and Autobiographies**—Students are often asked to write a book report on the biography or autobiography of a famous scientist. However, they often do so mechanically and do not benefit as much as we hope from the activity. Instead, reading excerpts about a scientist's life while studying a related topic may be more profitable. Students may be able to put themselves into science situations by reading about a person's thoughts and experiences at the time of an important discovery. Students may also be interested in learning about scientists as adolescents. A sample list of biographies is provided at the end of this chapter and in the Comic Books and Graphic Novels section that follows. Literature circles, discussed later in this chapter, can provide means for students to compare and contrast the lives of different scientists.

CHILDREN'S BOOKS

Children's books have often been looked down upon as a form of literature, and a common assumption is that it does not take real talent to write for children—that children's book authors are those who cannot "cut it" in the adult market. Nothing could be farther from the truth. There are good writers and bad writers at both levels. Children's books have an easier vocabulary and most have beautiful illustrations. They often address substantial and valuable content. Their simplicity and beauty can introduce a topic and generate inquiry. In an attempt to meet the needs of very young learners, science concepts may be occasionally oversimplified and actually promote misunderstandings or misinformation. Secondary students may be encouraged to verify the science presented in children's books and judge the books on science content. A classic children's book written in the 1930s, *Miss Pickerel Goes to Mars* by Ellen MacGregor, can be a clever way to introduce concepts of gravity and space travel.

Children's literature as an alternative to texts for English language learners (ELLs) is an option. Students could be asked to read and evaluate several children's books or to write a children's book explaining a science concept. Students could work with partners and write two versions of the book—one in English and another in the ELL's native language. In order to prevent students from being labeled as poor readers, whether for language or other reasons, all students can be required to review or use children's books. High-achieving students may be able to spot inadequacies of the books, appreciate the visual appeal of the books, and actually enjoy the challenge of writing children's books.

A book that can be quite effective in a unit on atomic energy is *Hiroshima No Pika* by Toschi Maruki (1982), which addresses the topics of radiation and atomic war. The story is based upon experiences of a family who survived the atomic attack on Hiroshima. Adult readers often react emotionally to the book and are not sure what level of students should use the book; they are shocked when they learn that it is actually a children's book used with primary children in Japan. The book is also thought provoking as some readers suggest that it is one sided in that it talks about the horrors of war from the Japanese viewpoint.

Finding appropriate children's books can be an adventure and has become a pastime for many secondary teachers who have built their own collections. Bookstores and libraries have special children's sections, and if one can balance on a tiny chair or get down on hands and knees, the view is quite enjoyable. Also, a librarian is an excellent source of information and will probably be very happy to see a scientist's interest. The National Science Teachers Association publishes lists of quality children's books related to science. The American Library Association and the International Reading Association also have helpful lists of children's and young adult books. Chapter 4 will provide more ideas for using children's books.

COMIC BOOKS AND GRAPHIC NOVELS

Some readers may remember hiding comic books inside other magazines or books at school because comic books were considered inappropriate or even "trash" reading. Comic books have an interesting and sometimes controversial history that dates back to the mid- and late 1800s. In the 1950s, the era of McCarthyism, an anti-comic book atmosphere existed and even Senate hearings were held. Perhaps this concern was somewhat justified due to some content. However, publishers began to self-regulate and developed a code to identify comics that are considered appropriate for young people.

Comic books are appealing to adolescents for many reasons. A prominent reason is that students are comfortable with visual media—television, movies, and computer graphics among the most apparent. Like children's books, comics can be used creatively in a science classroom. Comics can help students develop critical and analytic skills when they are studied for content and presentation (Versaci, 2001). Resources are available for teachers who might like to consider using comic books in their classrooms. Many organizations publish comic books especially designed for instructional purposes. The American Library Association Web site (http://www.ala.org) is a valuable resource if you want to learn more.

Closely related to comic books are graphic novels. This genre actually began as works for adults and Frans Nasereel, a Belgian, is often credited with coining the term. An American, Lynn Ward, wrote adult picture books in the 1930s. In 1992, Art Spiegelman's *Maus*, which is about the Holocaust, won a Pulitzer

Prize. The Japanese form of graphic novels, manga, has become very popular among adolescents. There are graphic novels particularly related to science. Jim Ottoviani (2001), an engineer, authored *Fallout*, a graphic novel about the development of the atomic bomb. Ottoviani is also the author of biographical graphic novels including *Dignifying Science: Stories About Women Scientists* (2003), *Two Fisted Science: Stories About Scientists* (2001), and *Suspended in Language: Niels Bohr's Life, Discoveries and the Century He Shaped* (2004). The Niels Bohr book could be combined with *Fallout* and the children's book, *Hiroshima No Pika*, in a physics class when discussing atomic power. Teachers may wish to read *Getting Graphic: Using Graphic Novels to Promote Literacy With Preteens and Teens* (Gorman and Smith, 2003). The book contains annotated lists, a guide to publishers, and hints for choosing graphic novels to use in classrooms.

POETRY

"Scientists observe with a clear eye, record their observations in precise, descriptive language, and craft their expressions. Poets do the same thing" (Cullinan, Scala, & Schroder, 1995, p. 72). What an interesting observation! You probably either love poetry or avoid it. Poetry is more than metered stanzas and rhyming words. Poetry can infuse science with an aesthetic quality that may touch even the most antiscience student. One of us, we won't say who, vehemently disliked science as a student and was completely turned off with the smell of labs and the hard glass of the test tubes until she could make a personal connection to what she was learning. Literature, including poetry, made that connection. Gary Paul Nabhan's book, *Cross-Pollinations: The Marriage of Science and Poetry* (2004), celebrates the aesthetic side of science. In an article in the *Journal of Geoscience Education,* Rule, Carnicelli, and Kane (2004) suggest that because much of science theory is abstract, scientists construct models and metaphors to explain phenomena. Poetry, with its use of metaphors, is a valuable tool that can help students make connections to science.

There are many sources for poems that could be used in science classes. A review of works of traditional poets who weren't scientists, such as Emily Dickinson, Robert Frost, and e. e. cummings, may provide thought-provoking poetry related to scientific themes. Shel Silverstein's books have several poems that may bring smiles to students. For instance, "Nope," about a microscope and a cantaloupe (Silverstein, 1996), is quite funny and could be used to encourage students to consider what microscopic bacteria might be present in food. *Verse and the Universe: Poems About Science and Mathematics* edited by Kurt Brown (1998) contains poetry by contemporary American poets and may appeal to more sophisticated readers.

NURSERY RHYMES AND CHILDREN'S SONGS

"Twinkle, twinkle little star, How I wonder what you are. . . . " From a very early age, children wonder about scientific phenomenon. What happens to their wonder as they progress through their school years? Perhaps using this rhyme to introduce a unit on the solar system or stars in astronomy or earth science class may make teenagers smirk at first, but after the initial tittering, the class could discuss what they think about stars and some of the scientists who followed through on their curiosity. A children's book, *Twinkle, Twinkle, Little Star,* illustrated by Sylvia Long (2001), reminds readers that nighttime travelers rely on stars to find their directions and may be fun to interject into a lesson.

Nursery rhymes have an interesting origin. According to some sources, many rhymes were actually political statements that were hidden in children's rhymes. Humpty Dumpty falling off a wall supposedly mocks a king. According to some sources, "Ring around the rosies . . . " refers to the black plague. Students could discuss the way diseases have been treated throughout history; they could address folklore and scientific treatments. This rhyme could be used in conjunction with books such as Preston's (1994) *The Hot Zone,* mentioned earlier (and discussed again with literature circles). The Web site Planet Science (http://www.planet-science.com/home.html) has a book of nursery rhyme science parodies that can be downloaded.

NEWSPAPERS AND POPULAR MAGAZINES

Newspapers can be the source of current events, weather, puzzles, cartoons, want ads, charts, and photographs. Teens, if they read the newspaper, often choose to read celebrity news or movie listings, fashion or sports stories, or horoscopes. With the increasing prevalence of online newspapers, however, more and more families are not having newspapers delivered regularly. The cost of home delivery may discourage some families to subscribe. Nevertheless, newspapers can be a valuable source of information and inspiration in the classroom.

Just as this section was being written, a wonderful headline appeared on the front page of the local paper: "Local Scientist's Humungous Fungus Verified by New Study" (Mavity, 2007). A paleobotanist who retired from the Smithsonian National Museum of Natural History studied protoaxites—organisms that predate dinosaurs—during his career. The scientist, Francis Hueber, theorized that the organisms were fungi, and his conclusions were recently verified by the University of Chicago. Think of the topics that could be discussed in local classrooms!

Many teachers keep a clipping file where they store just this kind of thing to enhance their teaching. The articles can be read aloud and discussed. Check the latest copyright laws, but if the article is new and just happens to fit into your lesson, you may be able to copy it and use it under the "fair use" provision. Keeping it and copying it again next year may violate copyright law unless you obtain permission to copy from the publisher; you can, of course, read from it.

Articles in magazines regularly pose questions that can be related to science. Hardly a week goes by that one doesn't find a newspaper article debating the existence of global warming. Magazines are favorites for adolescents. These magazines can range from entertainment or celebrity fan magazines to hobby magazines. Often, reluctant readers will not attempt a book but are willing to read magazines, and if the magazine is related to a special interest, they will struggle through difficult material. *Isaac Asimov's Science Fiction* magazine is quite popular among science fiction fans. We cannot overestimate the uses of such magazines as *Popular Science* or *Consumer Reports*. A lesson on the importance of verifying data could include a discussion of how tests are conducted for *Consumer Reports*. However, do not overlook magazines directed at teens, car or sports enthusiasts, or hobbyists. They may keep teachers abreast of current teen interests and may provide links between science and real life. Magazines and newspapers can be used at other stages in a 5E Model lesson design in addition to the Engage stage or the Expand phase of the 7E Model lesson design. Students can use them to gather data or compare their results with those published. Students can communicate science concepts by writing articles as suggested in Chapter 4.

BOOK TALKS

Time is valuable and you may not want to spend much of it on novels in your classroom. One way to introduce students to books on your topic is to do a book talk. A book talk takes only 5 to 10 minutes during which you try to arouse students' interest in a book and ultimately a science topic. If you find a book that intrigues you, share your enthusiasm with your students. Occasionally, students who have already read the book may add their thoughts. Your oral presentation can be expanded to include some artifacts related to the book (visual prompts). For instance, following a book talk on *The Hot Zone* (Preston, 1994), one might display articles about deadly viruses, a map showing areas impacted by the viruses, pictures of viruses, or biohazard icons. Include tapes or DVDs of movies such as *Outbreak* (1995) starring Dustin Hoffman, which was based on Preston's book, breathing masks, and antiseptics in your display. Since *Outbreak* is rated R, you may not want to actually view it in your class, but many students may choose to watch it on their own. You could also include newspaper clippings or magazine articles about the spread of bird flu. The steps in giving a book talk are quite simple:

Figure 3.1   Book Talk Strategy

1. Show the book to the class.

2. Tell a little about the author—background, other titles, etc.

3. Tell why you liked the book.

4. Read aloud a short passage to the students.

5. Ask if anyone has read the book.

6. If you wish, tell the students they may borrow your book. Otherwise, tell them where they can obtain copies.

7. Display the book prominently in your classroom.

Figure 3.2   Sample Book Talk: *The Hot Zone* by Richard Preston,
Anchor Books, New York, 1994

Because we are going to be talking about viruses in our next unit, I decided to share a book that I found quite exciting: THE HOT ZONE by Richard Preston. [Write title and author on board and show book.] Point out inside cover "From Deep in the Rain Forest, A Killer Virus Stalks the Human Race."

Richard Preston has written many books related to science. Some of them are based on actual events, and others are fiction. THE HOT ZONE is one of his books based on fact.

Richard Preston grew up near Boston and admits that he was not a very good student in high school. In fact, his grades were so bad that he had trouble getting into college. He says that he kept trying to get into college and was finally accepted. When he did get into college, he worked hard and actually graduated with honors. Later, he went to Princeton University, where he studied writing and learned that facts can be quite thrilling. He earned a doctorate in English. His first book, FIRST LIGHT, was about astronomy and he won an award for it from the American Physics Society.

He has two younger brothers. One brother is also an author, and the other brother is a doctor.

Richard Preston's newest book is about the redwood trees of California and is called THE WILD TREES. I will put a link to Richard Preston's Web page on our class Web page if you would like to read more about him (http://www .richardpreston.net).

Richard Preston says that he does a lot of research and checks his facts carefully when he is writing. I think that is why I like his books so much. They really make the facts exciting, and when I know that what he is writing about did or could happen, it makes me frightened in a way. It is said that when President Bill Clinton read one of Preston's books, he said it really frightened him, too.

I would like to read a short section of the book to you now. [Read pp. 197– 198.] "He saw something else in the pictures that left him frightened and filled with awe. . . . Because they were getting ready to burst."

[Talk about biology facts in the selection: virus cells shaped like threads, inclusion bodies.]

Has anyone in the class read this book? Did you like it? Why? Would you recommend it to your classmates?

The school library has two copies of this book. I told the librarian that students in my class may want to borrow them, so she put them on reserve. All you need to do is ask at the desk if you wish to sign out one. I also have two copies myself that you can borrow. It is also available at the bookstore downtown. Mine cost $7.99.

Be sure to check out the Web link for Richard Preston!

LITERATURE CIRCLES

We do know that many students say they are turned off when they are forced to read something. We also know that adolescents like to make choices and have some control over what they do. A strategy that can be used to incorporate books into the curriculum, conserve valuable class time, and allow students choices is literature circles. In the last section, *The Hot Zone* was suggested for a book talk. That same book could also be used for literature circles. Richard Preston wrote three books related to "dark biology" according to his Web site (Preston, 2008): *The Hot Zone, The Cobra Event* (1999), and *The Demon in the Freezer: A True Story* (2002). *The Cobra Event* is a fictional story about the possibility of a bioterrorist attack in New York City. *The Demon in the Freezer: A True Story* is about bioterrorism and smallpox. Imagine the discussions that could evolve from reading these books. Some of the activities could include identifying the science facts related to the diseases mentioned in each book, identifying methods to deal with bio-hazardous materials, identifying the ways that diseases can spread, and the impact that the crises had upon the scientists involved. After finishing the books, groups could share the information about their diseases and then compare and contrast the information.

Figure 3.3   Literature Circles Strategy

1. Choose several books related to a topic of different genres and reading levels. The number of books depends upon the size of your class and the number of groups you establish.

2. Divide each book into an equivalent number of sections (four is a good number). The sections should be comparable in size; make divisions at logical places. The number of sections should be equivalent to the number of class periods you plan to devote to the book. Perhaps choose to use the books on Fridays, four weeks in a row. Then have a group sharing time on the fifth Friday. If you traditionally give a "Friday quiz," you could use time after the quiz for your literature circles.

3. Develop "generic" worksheets related to each section to be used pre-, during, and post-reading. Refer to Chapter 2 for ideas.

4. Introduce the books by a book talk during which you give a quick overview of each.

5. Have students write the book titles in order of preference. Tell the students that you will group them according to their book choices and hopefully everyone will get a first- or second-choice book.

6. Divide students into groups; each person will have a job within the group. Jobs can rotate for each class period or be adjusted based on students' needs or your objectives. Some jobs could be Vocabulary Detective, Summarizer, Questioner, Fact Detector, Illustrator, Time Keeper, or Character Analyzer.

7. Explain the jobs and assignments. Depending upon the students and curriculum needs, students can read the material outside of class. Some teachers require students to bring their books every day and to read them silently at opportune times.

8. Have students discuss the books in small groups at the prescribed times. You can devote a class period or perhaps just part of a period each time. Students will be personally responsible for worksheets and preparing information related to their jobs.

9. While students are participating in their discussion groups, circulate and offer provocative questions. Help students make inferences, ask their own questions, or draw conclusions.

10. Plan a time for students to share information about their books to the rest of the class. This could be in any format—oral reports, posters, Web pages, or bulletin boards. Often, students will want to read a book based upon the recommendations of their classmates. Talk about how the book relates to the overall theme.

SUMMARY

Often, students are willing to interact with content in nontraditional ways and this motivation may actually increase their knowledge. Adolescents like to make choices and have fun. They also appreciate teachers who are in tune with their interests (Chamberlain, 2003). The suggestions we have made can be incorporated into inquiry-based units—students can develop their inquiry questions, see how science is applied in society, and learn about different ways science content can be communicated. Combinations of fiction, nonfiction, and poetry can serve to ground science instruction and keep motivation high. Close your eyes and visualize one of your classes. What do your students look like? Are they children from Garrison Keillor's Lake Wobegon (all above average)? Do they all share the same interest in science? We are responsible for all students; student diversity makes life as a teacher interesting and sometimes frustrating. Of particular concern to many secondary teachers is the inclusion of students with special needs in content area classes. Gender, language, racial, ethnic, and socioeconomic differences create another set of needs. The wide range of student needs can be met by using a wide variety of materials. We have made a few suggestions, but the number of possibilities is endless—combine your interests and those of your students and you will probably come up with even better ideas. In the next chapter, we will show how reading and writing can be combined to enrich your classrooms even more.

SELECTED BOOKS FOR SCIENCE

Astronomy and Physics

Berman, Bob. (1995). *Secrets of the Night Sky: The Most Amazing Things in the Universe You Can See With the Naked Eye.* New York: William Morrow.

Berman explains the sky in easy-to-understand terms. He addresses such topics as the effect of time and longitude and latitude on what we see, how the constellations we see change according to the seasons, and the way constellations are mapped.

Berman, Bob. (2003). *Strange Universe: The Weird and Wild Science of Everyday Life—On Earth and Beyond.* New York: Henry Holt.

Berman's book provides information that would be interesting additions to astronomy and physics lessons. The author discusses a range of topics from "blue moons" to northern lights. The easy-to-understand language cleverly explains scientific phenomena that interest scientists and laypeople alike.

Jargodski, Christopher P., & Potter, Franklin. (2001). *Mad About Physics: Braintwisters, Paradoxes, and Curiosities.* New York: Wiley.

This is one of those how-does-it-work books that will be a great addition to a classroom library. The applications to real life are fun and informative. A list of references is included.

Krauss, Lawrence M. (1995). *The Physics of Star Trek.* New York: HarperCollins.

In the foreword to this book, Stephen Hawking states, "Science fiction like Star Trek is not just good fun but it also serves a serious purpose, that of expanding the human imagination" (p. xi). Students may be interested in learning about how, or if, technology used in the TV shows and movies works. The book presents examples and related physics laws.

Macaulay, David. (2000). *Building Big.* Boston: Houghton Mifflin.

This book was a companion to the PBS series of the same name. In it, the principles and functions of architectural structures are examined. Diagrams explain forces that work on structures such as compression and tension in bridges and water pressure on dams. Structures discussed include bridges, dams, tunnels, domes, and skyscrapers.

Preston, Richard. (1996). *First Light: The Search for the Edge of the Universe.* New York: Random House.

First Light is the story of astronomers who had vision and determination. It also shows astronomers as people who have lives and conflicts but still make fascinating discoveries. It is the story of the Hale Telescope—how it came to be. Preston, an award-winning author, also penned *The Hot Zone* recommended in the Biology section of this list.

Biology/Ecology

Beebe, William. (1988). *The Book of Naturalists: An Anthology of the Best Natural History.* Princeton, NJ: Princeton University Press.

Originally published in 1944, the book contains writings of naturalists throughout history from Aristotle to Rachel Carson. It gives readers the opportunity to use primary sources by reprinting selections from books and journals.

Carson, Rachel. (1967). *Silent Spring.* New York: Fawcett.

This seminal work originally published in 1962 is credited for starting the environmental movement and pointing out the hazards of chemicals that enter the ecosystem.

Nabhan, Gary Paul. (2004). *Cross-Pollinations: The Marriage of Science and Poetry.* Minneapolis, MN: Milkweed Editions.

Don't let the title fool you. This book addresses much more than poetry in the traditional sense. Readers can gain insight into the scientific method, culture and science, and the development of a scientist. Nabhan is a scientist, writer, and artist who skillfully blends his interests to present a rich and intriguing look at ethnobiology (a combination of ecology and anthropology).

Preston, Richard. (1995). *The Hot Zone.* New York: Anchor Books.

This book was recommended to us by an undergraduate biology student. It is based upon a true story of the progress and study of a deadly virus. It's one you can't put down as it brings possibilities to the surface that we might not consider.

Thompson, Jennifer A. (2007). *Seeds for the Future: The Impact of Genetically Modified Crops on the Environment.* Ithaca, NY: Comstock.

This book tackles the issue of genetic engineering through discussions of environmental hazards, the effects of biodiversity of genetic engineering, regulations, and biosafety related to genetic engineering and other thought-provoking questions. This would be a good resource for science, technology, and society discussions.

Weiner, Jonathan. (1995). *The Beak of the Finch.* New York: Vintage.

The Galápagos Islands, Darwin, and birds—combine these with two scientists who devote their careers to studying them and you have an engaging story. The book not only discusses theory, but it also shows how scientists can strive to learn more. The book also presents an excellent example of methods for data collection and analysis. The book was a Pulitzer Prize winner.

Chemistry

Karukstis, Kerry K., & Van Hecke, Gerald. (2003). *Chemistry Connections: The Chemical Basis of Everyday Phenomena* (2nd ed.). San Diego, CA: Academic Press.

Why do carbonated beverages go flat when they get warm? This is just one of the many topics discussed in this fascinating look at how chemistry impacts almost everything around us. In a question-and-answer format, chemistry principles are explained in easy-to-understand terms.

McGee, Harold. (2004). *On Food and Cooking: The Science and Lore of the Kitchen.* New York: Scribner.

For those who like to cook or to eat, this book is fascinating. It explains the science behind many of the common processes in food preparation, such as fermentation and preservation of meat. Other topics range from how the cells in potatoes determine the texture to why heating intensifies the flavor of some fruits and vegetables.

Stocker, Jack H. (1998). *Chemistry and Science Fiction.* Washington, DC: American Chemical Society.

Science fiction is a popular genre among adolescents. According to this book, many scientists were motivated in their career choices because of science fiction. This text discusses the evolution of science fiction and gives specific examples of stories and books that incorporate chemistry in the plot. The book is a great resource for chemistry teachers and may interest science fiction fans.

BIOGRAPHIES AND
INTERDISCIPLINARY BOOKS

Aczel, Amir D. (2003). *Pendulum: Léon Foucault and the Triumph of Science.* New York: Atria Books.

The pendulum . . . we often take it for granted. Foucault's story will engage readers and encourage them to consider possibilities. The biography also discusses his other interests and discoveries, including color theory, heat waves, and the speed of light. A good read.

Berlinski, David. (2000). *Newton's Gift: How Sir Isaac Newton Unlocked the System of the World.* New York: The Free Press.

The reader will find a biography enriched with mathematical formulas and scientific explanations. Newton's life is presented from childhood through his discovery periods.

Capra, Fritojof. (2007). *The Science of Leonardo: Inside the Mind of the Great Genius of the Renaissance.* New York: Doubleday.

A great book for interdisciplinary connections with art, history, and mathematics. Capra presents da Vinci as a "systematic thinker" far ahead of his time and discusses many of da Vinci's detailed drawings, ranging from the mechanisms of the arms to architectural designs. Capra is also the author of *Tao of*

Physics (1975), an interesting read that connects modern physics with Eastern philosophies.

Johnson, George. (2005). *Miss Leavitt's Stars: The Untold Story of the Woman Who Discovered How to Measure the Universe.* New York: Atlas Books.

Although more information about Leavitt's life would be interesting, the author states that because she was a woman in a man's field at the beginning of the 20th century, her importance was overlooked. We do know that she was well educated but was not awarded a degree (only available to men at that time). She was a "computer," the term used for number crunchers in scientific laboratories, whose work with numbers produced results that were used by many.

Kjelle, Marylou Morano. (2005). *Antoine Lavoiser: Father of Modern Chemistry.* New York: Mitchell Lane.

Oxygen is fundamental in chemistry and biology. This book tells the tale of the man who made the world understand its significance. Lavoiser survived the turmoil of the French Revolution to become one of science's all-time leaders. Students may like to learn about his work in this historical perspective. The book may also be used to make interdisciplinary connections with social studies.

Lear, Linda (1997). *Rachel Carson. Witness for a Nation.* New York: Henry Holt.

This is a rather thick but thorough book that traces Carson's life from childhood through her battle to join the scientific community, which limited access to women. It provides a deep discussion of the environmental battles that plagued society in the mid-20th century. Carson confronted government and industry in her environmental campaign. This book provides interesting background information for discussions of global warming and similar science, technology, and society discussion.

FROM OUR CHILDREN'S BOOKSHELVES

Bingham, Caroline, Morgan, Ben, & Robertson, Matthew (Editors). (2007). *Buzz: What's All the Buzz About These Bugs?* New York: DK Publishing.

This colorful book is filled with science information and may be missed by those not looking in children's sections of bookstores. It would be a wonderful companion to the arthropod study mentioned in this book. Vocabulary is presented clearly and thoroughly with examples, photographs, and diagrams. The book addresses questions such as How do you tell apart different kinds of arthropods? What is an insect? Why are wings important? What are the different kinds of wings? How do insects see? How did the cochineal change the politics of Europe? How are insects used in crime scene investigations? What are different careers that work with arthropods? This book is a must on a biology teacher's shelf! The vocabulary and concept development produce a junior-senior high readability.

Fisher, Aileen. (2001). *Sing of the Earth and Sky: Poems About Our Planet and the Wonders Beyond.* Honesdale, PA: Boyds Mills.

Children's poems about the earth, moon, sun, and stars. The poems are humorous and muse about the phenomena. The short-and-sweet poems embody the curiosity of children.

Jay, Lorraine A. (2000). *Sea Turtles.* Minnetonka, MN: Northwood.

Although written for younger children, the photographs in this small book are magnificent and make it worthwhile for inclusion in a high school teacher's collection. The book discusses different species of sea turtles that are found in the coastal United States and their usual habitat. The book uses scientific vocabulary and emphasizes science facts. A list of Internet sites related to sea turtles is included.

Lauber, Patricia. (1986). *Volcano: The Eruption and Healing of Mount St. Helens.* New York: Harcourt Brace.

The book details the progression of the eruption with photographs, diagrams, and maps. Before-and-after pictures of the location provide graphic evidence of the impact of volcanoes. A chapter addresses life that survived and colonized the area after the eruption. The book, found in a children's section, has a readability of approximately eighth grade.

Lewis, J. Patrick. (2004). *Scien-Trickery: Riddles in Science.* New York: Harcourt.

The book contains 18 science-related riddles in rhyme formats. Topics include many that may be discussed in science—gravity, chemistry, electricity, magnetism, sound, astronomy, and biology with titles such as "Push Me, Pull Me" and "Revealing Ceiling." Although the riddles are not profound, they could be use on bulletin boards or written on the chalkboard as students come into class. The book does have a page of science explanations.

Macaulay, David. (1988). *The Way Things Work.* Boston: Houghton Mifflin.

Another great reference book that will answer students when they ask, "Why do we need to learn this?" The diagrams help explain some complex ideas in simple terms. There is also a section that puts science ideas in a historical perspective.

Willis, Nancy Carol. (2006). *Red Knot: A Shorebird's Incredible Journey.* Middletown, DE: Birdsong Books.

I chose this book because I live in Delaware, where the Red Knots feed on the eggs of the Horseshoe Crabs. Local crabbers and environmentalists are often at odds, especially during the Red Knot season. However, the contents are excellent for those studying the migration of birds. The book traces a year in the life of a Red Knot from Tierra del Fuego in southernmost Chile to Southampton Island in the Northwest Territories of Canada. The book is fact filled and beautifully illustrated by the author. Short sentence lengths make this book have a lower-grade readability; however, the concepts are of a higher level.

SELECTED TRADE BOOKS MENTIONED IN THIS CHAPTER

The Chocolate War – Robert Cormier
The Cobra Event – Richard Preston
Demon in the Freezer: A True Story – Richard Preston
Dignifying Science: Stories About Women Scientists – Jim Ottoviani
Dracula – Bram Stoker
Dragon series – Jane Yolen
Fallout – Jim Ottoviani
The Forensic Casebook – Ngaire E. Genge
Frankenstein – Mary Shelley
The Giver – Lois Lowry
The Grapes of Wrath – John Steinbeck
Hiroshima No Pika – Toshi Maruki
The House of the Scorpion – Nancy Farmer
How to Dunk a Doughnut – Len Fisher
Journey to the Center of the Earth – Jules Verne
Jurassic Park – Michael Crichton
Lord of the Rings – J. R. R. Tolkien
Maus – Art Spiegelman
Miss Pickerel Goes to Mars – Ellen MacGregor
Out of the Dust – Karen Hesse
The Outsiders – S. E. Hinton
Phineas Gage: A Gruesome Tale of Brain Science – John Fleischman
The Pigman – Paul Zindel
Pit Dragon series – Jane Yolen
Science and Medical Discoveries: Cloning – Nancy Harris
The Science of Harry Potter – Roger Highfield
The Science of Sherlock Holmes – E. J. Wagner
Suspended in Language: Niels Bohr's Life, Discoveries,
*   and the Century He Shaped* – J. Ottoviani
The Time Machine – H. G. Wells
Twinkle, Twinkle, Little Star – Sylvia Long
Two Fisted Science: Stories About Scientists – Jim Ottoviani
War of the Worlds – H. G. Wells
The Wild Trees – Richard Preston
A Wrinkle in Time – Madeleine L'Engle

WEB SITES REFERENCED

American Library Association – http://www.ala.org
Planet Science – http://www.planet-science.com
Richard Preston – http://www.richardpreston.net

Figure 3.4   Tips for a Literacy-Rich Classroom

1. Have a variety of print materials available for students to use.

2. Use key vocabulary liberally on bulletin boards, posters, or walls.

3. Encourage students to contribute materials that they find.

4. Have reading materials with a wide range of reading levels available.

5. Model effective reading strategies.

6. Read aloud to your students regularly.

7. Display reading materials in creative ways.

8. Have fun with vocabulary words. Play games or use puzzles.

9. Use many types of materials such as poetry, nonfiction, fiction, newspapers, magazines, or children's books.

10. Include writing activities regularly.

11. Create your own classroom library. Supplement it with books borrowed from the library that relate to current units or themes.

12. Share your enthusiasm for literature and writing.

4

Writing in Science

What kinds of writing do you do in your daily life? Do you make lists, write personal or business letters, write e-mail messages, fill out forms, or write lesson plans? Writing is a form of communication that we often take for granted; yet when asked to write in an academic setting, we (and our students) may be hesitant. Students often do not like to write because they believe that they don't have anything important to say. Some students may be afraid to put their own words on paper for fear of criticism. Others don't like to write because they are bored with the same type of assignments year after year. So, as teachers, we have challenges ahead of us.

If you are like many secondary science teachers, you may have five or more classes a day (with more than one preparation to do). Each class may have as many as 30 students. You have labs to set up, tests to make and grade, lessons to prepare, computer problems, standards-based lesson plans to submit, meetings to attend, and now they are telling you that you must incorporate writing in your lessons. The powers that be tell you that writing is important; No Child Left Behind Act and the new SAT writing component are used as arguments.

You may agree that some writing may be important. You've tried the research report routine; the students hate it and you get tired of grading those reports that all seem alike and sound like encyclopedia entries. Teachers can develop purposeful and motivating methods for students to write and share their writing. In this chapter, we will explore the theoretical arguments for incorporating writing in the science classroom, types of writing strategies that may be used, and possibilities for assessing content knowledge through writing. We hope to provide you with some ideas that may interest you and your students and that will be manageable in the context of your content area expectations.

You probably know a good deal about writing; you may be able to identify some of your own roadblocks to writing. You may also remember writing assignments that you liked and those you didn't. Think about the questions in Figure 4.1 as you consider incorporating writing into your curriculum.

Figure 4.1   Questions Before Starting Writing Projects

1. **Who are my students?** What writing experiences and skills do they bring with them? What are their interests? What are their strengths and weaknesses? Are there cultural or linguistic differences that may impede their success? Are there cultural or linguistic differences that may be assets to their experiences and the experiences of their classmates?

2. **What content** is important for them to know and be able to communicate?

3. **What are the objectives or standards** for my classes that may have some relationship with writing?

4. **Where might I find time** in my schedule to incorporate writing? Should I have several small projects or one large project?

5. **What resources** are available to the students for their research and completion of the project?

6. **What kind of writing interests me?**

7. **What kinds of writing do scientists actually do?**

Start your own writer's notebook about science. When you think of a topic or even a crazy idea, write it down. When you think of a particular play on words that intrigues you or you hear a joke that makes you think of a science idea, write it down. Don't worry about writing in complete sentences or even spelling words correctly. The notebook will be your personal brainstorming tool. When you are trying to decide on a writing project or even a prompt for your students, revisit your notebook. Show the notebook to your students. You do not have to show them what is in it; just show that you use it. An excellent guide for those who are considering the use of a writer's notebook is Ralph Fletcher's *A Writer's Notebook* (1996). Teachers who model writing themselves can share their own writing or guide the students as they read different forms of writing done by others.

WHY WRITING?

The use of language in developing science literacy for many years was not considered primary. Manipulating physical objects and using logic was the focus of early science education programs such as the Science—A Process Approach (SAPA) popular in the 1970s (Klein, 2006). This author used the program for middle school science during that era and remembers doing the activities with students. We worked with the scientific method, recorded data, and drew conclusions. However, communication of student ideas wasn't paramount in the process. Students completed "experiments" defined by the program according to specified procedures and drew conclusions that were expected. During standard lab exercises, students responded to questions prepared in advance with predictable answers. Communication was often student to teacher. If group work was included in the lesson, students followed prescribed procedures or discussed "right answers." Klein (2006) asserts that language "was viewed as a by-product of thought, rather than a contributor to it" (p. 149).

Oral communication during an inquiry lesson provides students with the opportunity to share and construct knowledge together; this is consistent with the social constructivist perspective. Students pose questions, compare ideas, and suggest alternatives. They explain their ideas to each other. Writing is an extension of this process. Writing following discussion leads to greater achievement than writing-only or talking-only activities (Hohenshell & Hand, 2006; Klein, 2006).

It is difficult to separate reading and writing: both are literary processes. When we add the concept of science literacy to the mix, we consider how reading and writing can lead to our students' content knowledge and ability to communicate in a scientific community. Through writing, students can explore the nature of science, the processes of science, their attitudes toward science, and the relationships between science and society. They can also reflect upon their understanding of science content and the skills that were necessary for them to achieve their learning. When writing is combined with reading, students' learning can grow exponentially.

Two distinct roles have been identified for writing in high school science. Writing is a form of communication through which students may show their understanding of science concepts, their reasoning strategies, and how they came to understandings through activities; it becomes a record of their acquisition of scientific knowledge. Additionally, through writing, students can clarify their learning and manipulate their ideas. This second role of writing allows students to write for different purposes and audiences in addition to contributing to their own knowledge (Prain, 2006).

To be effective, writing-to-learn approaches depend upon the type of writing expected, the methods through which the writing is produced, the audience for whom the writing is intended, the topics chosen, and the sources of information used. Writing that requires reasoning appears to produce more learning than activities that just require paraphrasing. Tasks that require students to synthesize information from a variety of sources and are directed toward real-life audiences appear to promote learning (Klein, 2006).

Writing is an active process. It involves cognition and communication. A variety of strategies that scaffold students' thinking may include pre-writing activities that encourage students to make connections between concepts. They must make many decisions about what they will write and how they will write the information. They must consider their audiences: who will be reading the information and for what purpose (Hohenshell & Hand, 2006)?

Students may also appreciate others' work while reading when they have had experiences expressing their own ideas through writing. As the pieces of writing are discussed, teachers can help students notice the techniques that other writers have used to express ideas and get validation for their own ideas.

Students can learn to understand different approaches to sharing science information and the process scientists go through when writing their findings. Investigating the writing process and learning to present ideas and supporting details can help students become more critical readers of others' work.

Students seem to benefit from language-based activities involving writing explanations, even without advanced planning. They do not seem to be disadvantaged by working in heterogeneous groups for writing. Sequencing writing from spontaneous writing to genre-based assignments appears to be most productive. Writing appears to help weaker students as much as it does high-achieving students; talking before writing is better (Rivard, 2004).

TYPES OF WRITING

In our daily experiences, we encounter different types of writing. Newspapers, atlases, and encyclopedias are examples of informational or declarative writing. Persuasive writing, work that argues and attempts to convince the reader about an idea, is found all around us in editorials or advertisements. Environmental issues make good topics for this type of writing. When actually writing to community or political groups, it gives the task meaning. Creative writing entertains us. Technical writing tells us how to program our VCRs or cell phones. These are all examples of formal writing. The types of writing may overlap somewhat—a persuasive piece may be very creative.

Informal writing projects encourage students to transition between speech and writing and give students opportunities to communicate in a nonthreatening format. These informal types may include individual reflection journals in which students can write freely, often without sharing with other students or even the teacher. Such writing may not always be learning experiences by themselves, but they may engage cognitive processes that may lead to learning (Klein, 2006). Informal writing can be especially helpful because students can write their thoughts without worrying about grammar and spelling. They can write all or partially in their native languages and then translate their thoughts when they convert their ideas to more formal writing assignments.

Writing projects, like reading assignments, are more effective if they engage the students in meaningful ways. Students who see a purpose for an activity are more likely to complete it. The design of the project can be modified to meet the needs of both students and curriculum standards. Assignments may be varied by format, cognitive demands (level of thinking—high order or low order; type of thinking—inductive or deductive), directions, affective demands, or complexity of language. In the following sections, we will look at informal and formal writing tasks, types of writing including scientific writing, and the benefits of the activities.

INFORMAL WRITING TASKS

Informal writing tasks provide students with opportunities to make personal connections with what they observe or read. Usually, the audience for informal writing is the student or perhaps a partner; thus the act of writing is less threatening. Students are able to connect new information to their prior knowledge. Students may become comfortable mixing scientific or technical vocabulary within their personal conversation styles or dialects. Within an informal format, students may express their own confusions or understandings; they may begin to express their reasoning and inferences. If the teacher does read and respond to informal writing tasks, an opportunity to establish a dialogue can arise. Teachers who respond are able to create an atmosphere for risk taking by acknowledging students' thoughts and opinions without evaluation. Responses may include, "This is an interesting perspective on the question" or "I'd like to hear more about your thinking" or "Could you explain this idea to me?" Teacher responses can encourage students to reconsider ideas or clarify their own thinking. In essence, through responses teachers may encourage students and lead them to a more formal writing style. Furthermore, when students have motivation to explain their ideas to a receptive audience, they may want to express themselves clearly.

During informal writing, grammar and spelling are not an issue although these may be addressed. Typically, informal writing is not graded except for perhaps participation in the activity; they could be included in students' portfolios to document growth. Nevertheless, informal writing can be an excellent vehicle for assessment of student progress toward a goal. Teachers can determine if students understand concepts, if they have misconceptions or confusions, or if students are able to define problems or issues.

Informal writing can take many forms. Many times, it is difficult to separate reading and writing activities. Informal writing may be used in conjunction with pre-reading, during reading, or post-reading activities or with investigations requiring data creation and analysis. If you refer back to Chapters 2 and 3, you can see where writing was integrated. Below are several examples of informal writing activities that may be adapted for different purposes by the teacher.

The Think-Write-Share-Write activity is similar to the Think-Pair-Share activity recommended for cooperative learning. The Think-Write-Share-Write extends the concept of discussions (talk) to writing. It can also be modified to stop the activity after sharing instead of asking students to go back and edit; encouraging students to edit at this point can help when students are later asked to do more formal writing.

Figure 4.2   Think-Write-Share-Write Strategy

This activity encourages students to communicate their ideas with a partner—a step in social construction of knowledge. Students write a response to an activity or question, then they share the information with a partner. The partner may ask for clarification of the idea or may ask a follow-up question. The student goes back and rewrites the response if necessary. This gives a student practice in editing his or her written work but in a nonthreatening, informal setting. The student knows he or she has an audience; often, it is easier for students to share their writing with a peer than a teacher.

Example: Students are given dilemma cards that allow them to explore their feelings about ways humans interact and possibly harm the environment. They then communicate their ideas as to what they would do. Their partner helps them clarify their beliefs and see how their actions can affect various situations.

The Learning Log strategy addresses several issues that may inhibit students' writing. First, the prompts are nonthreatening. Students have control over what they put down. They are not answering informational questions that you asked. Also, students can sense that you think their ideas are important. When you ask them to tell you what they would like to learn, you are asking

Figure 4.3   Learning Log Activity

At the end of each class session, students are asked to reflect upon what they did and what they learned. These learning logs may be kept in a notebook or computer file. Students may use them to review what they learned as they begin the next class; they may also reflect upon their entire inquiry process at the end of a unit. The following are some prompts to start their log entries:

Something I learned today was _____.
Something that confuses me is _____.
Something that surprised me was _____.
Something I would like to learn more about is _____.
A personal connection I made was _____.
If I could ask a scientist something about today's topic, I'd ask _____.

them for advice. For you, the activity provides an excellent closure activity in your lesson plan. The activity takes only a few minutes, but you can glean a good deal of information when you review students' responses. First, did students get the main points of your lesson? Were there misconceptions? Is there something that interests the students that you could include in a future lesson? When you address their confusions and interests and let them know that you are addressing the issues they raised, you are acknowledging the importance of what they have to say. Their responses could be an excellent source for future inquiry activities.

The method is easy to manage. You can have prepared forms for the students to use or you can have students hand in their answers on notebook paper as they leave the room. You can review their answers in 5–10 minutes, make quick notes for yourself or on their papers, and return their papers the next class period. The papers do not need to be graded; in fact, it may be better not to grade them. Students may feel freer to write if the papers are not graded.

An alternative way to use the method is to have students keep their answers in a notebook or computer file which you will collect on a regular basis. You may want to collect them each week or just before you review for a test. If you have five classes a day, you could collect one group's notebooks on Monday, the second group's notebooks on Tuesday, and so on. It is entirely up to you. From the notebooks, you could compile a list of common questions and include these in your review session. If the responses are kept in a computer file, students could e-mail the files to you at designated times in the unit or print out a hard copy for you. This way, the students will still be able to keep their files to use on their own. The following strategies take very little time out of a class period, yet they can provide valuable information so the teacher can learn about students' content knowledge and confusions.

Figure 4.4   Pose a Question Strategy

Students write questions on index cards and give the questions to the teacher. Teachers can then incorporate students' questions in the next day's lesson or use the questions as a review of material. Students may be asked to write their names on the cards; however, the teacher may choose not to reveal the name of the writer. This activity encourages students to pose and write questions carefully that they may not want to ask in a large group. Additionally, because the teacher is the audience, students may be more likely to want to be more careful about their writing skills.

Interactive Note Taking is similar to the Cornell note-taking method mentioned in Chapter 2; instead of just a method to use during reading of a selection, it can be adapted to use during experimental activities.

Figure 4.5   One-Minute Paper Strategy

Students write for 1 minute at the end of a class period or an activity. The teacher collects the papers and uses them to assess what students learned and to determine misconceptions. The papers can be returned to the students. Students can review their thoughts at the beginning of the next class period. If the teacher responds to the papers, students can get feedback about their ideas. If students keep their papers in a notebook, they can see the development of their ideas over time. One-minute papers are similar to the learning logs, but instead of prompts, the students can write more freely. Teachers may use these as formative assessments to adjust forthcoming lessons if necessary.

Figure 4.6   Interactive Note-Taking Strategy

This strategy is used while students are experimenting, collecting data, discussing a topic, or reading. Notebook paper is divided into two columns. In the first column, students write a bit of information; in the second column, students ask questions or make personal connections to the information. Students are creating a dialogue with the information (Chesbro, 2006).

SOURCE: Adapted from Chesbro, R. (2006). Using interactive notebooks for inquiry-based science. *Science Scope. 29*(7), 30–34.

Figure 4.7   Interactive Note-Taking Sample

Dissolving salt in distilled water
Data collected February 25, 2006

My observations	My questions
We had 1 liter of water at 38 degrees C.	What would happen with warmer water?
We added 2 tablespoons of salt.	I wonder what would happen if we added more salt?
The temperature dropped about 2 degrees.	I wonder what would happen if we started with colder water?

Figure 4.7 shows a portion of interactive note taking during an inquiry lesson. In this example, students participate in an activity during which salt is dissolved in distilled water. The note taking includes data collected. Students record their observations and write questions that they personally develop. This encourages students to observe carefully and consider different ideas related to what they see. Their note taking could then be used in class discussions and to formulate inquiry projects.

Each of these activities takes little preparation and practically no additional class time; the activities can be integrated easily into a reading or inquiry lesson. If teachers do choose to read and respond to students' writing, some planning and organization may be needed. However, incorporating informal writing regularly, if not daily, may enhance student learning and lead to better formal writing. Prain and Hand (1999) suggest that the role of reflective writing through which students consider how their writing enhances their learning cannot be underestimated.

FORMAL WRITING TASKS

Over the last two decades, types of formal writing that could be included in secondary science classes have been debated. One group of theorists suggests that students should be required to write as scientists write even if the writing is simplified. The assertion is that students need this kind of writing to be scientifically literate. This group contends that because science writing is so different from everyday language, students need explicit teaching in the form. They propose that everyday language is vague and imprecise and it is not possible to explain scientific knowledge in common language (Hildebrand, 1998; Prain, 2006).

The other view of writing in science suggests that the strength of other genres of writing in science class is that scientific knowledge is presented in common language. Proponents of this view ask, should science writing be the only acceptable way to convey science knowledge and to provide entrance into the science community (Hildebrand, 1998)? Those who hold this perspective suggest that nonscientific language enables students to make connections between their scientific knowledge and their everyday lives. These theorists support the social constructivist perspective of learning. Using such techniques as analogies, metaphors, or similes to compare science concepts to their everyday lived experiences enables students to understand the science concepts on a deeper level (Hildebrand, 1998; Prain, 2006).

Hand, Prain, Lawrence, and Yore (1999) suggest that the second view is consistent with the interpretation of scientific literacy as proposed by the National Research Council. Students, according to this perspective, are supposed to be able to present their scientific knowledge to different audiences using different writing types; this expands the concept of science literacy. Students in a classroom are not the same as a research team of scientists, thus pure scientific writing is not a necessity (Hand & Prain, 2002). Some recent research (Gunel, Hand, & Gunduz, 2006) suggests that students' understanding is enhanced when they share their learning in different forms of communication.

Formal writing tasks often produce angst among students and teachers. Students, as mentioned previously, might be reluctant to put their thoughts in writing for others to see, and teachers are concerned about how to grade the writing—should they worry about grammar, spelling, or content? Teachers are also concerned that time spent on writing detracts from content learning. In this section, we will discuss types of formal writing, ways to encourage students and motivate them to write, and possibilities for assessment and evaluation of the products and science content knowledge.

Students may have been introduced to process writing in other classes. Process writing strategies with specific and sequential steps (pre-writing, draft, editing, rewriting, and publishing) are often presented as *the* way to compose writing and can often be stifling and intimidating to students. Students are probably familiar with the five-paragraph essay in which the first paragraph is their introduction, the last paragraph is their conclusion and the middle three paragraphs are main ideas and supporting details. Unfortunately, many students have interpreted this strategy to be the only way to write an essay, just as they believe that a lab report is the only way to share what they have learned in science.

Formal tasks can include narratives about a topic or experience that define an issue, explain a procedure, analyze data, propose a hypothesis, or defend a conclusion. Different purposes lend themselves to different formats. First, we will discuss informational discipline-based writing; much writing in science follows a heuristic or pattern. When students engage in any kind of formal writing tasks, they are asked to

- Identify an audience for their writing: Are they writing for a scientist, their teacher, other students, younger students, or the general public?
- Identify their purpose for writing: Is it to explain, describe, inform, persuade, or entertain?
- Choose a format for their writing: Is it a lab report, research project, newspaper article, essay, children's book, story, or poem?
- Identify the characteristics and parameters of the format.
- Choose a perspective for writing: pro or con; first, second, or third person.
- Decide what information will be included.
- Verify information and/or prepare arguments.
- Draft, edit, and publish their work.

It may be easy to consider these tasks as a recipe to be followed sequentially; however, the nature of inquiry and publishing information related to the inquiry may suggest a different pattern. For instance, students may decide what information they wish to share, then determine an audience or format that would be the most interesting or motivational to use. On the other hand, they may be given a task to present their information to a particular audience and need to decide on the method to use. Furthermore, they may be drafting their information during the inquiry process and may need to edit the information only at the end.

Formal Scientific Writing

Formal scientific writing is argumentation. Scientists want to persuade readers to accept their conclusions. Examples of this kind of writing are articles in scientific journals. The writer makes claims and then provides data as evidence to support his or her claim. Meeting the expectations of the audience is crucial. Other scientists must be convinced that the author's conclusions are logical results of accurate data analysis. For this reason, clear guidelines are used and reviewers and editors of journals expect clear, direct connections between the data and the conclusions (Yore, Hand, & Prain, 2002).

Secondary students are usually not expected to write such sophisticated journal articles; typically their writing takes the form of lab reports. However, lab reports have been criticized for not requiring students to think deeply about their activities. In some cases, lab reports ask students to do little more than fill in the blanks or write short narrative sentences.

Elements of good scientific writing include precision, clarity, and brevity; the writing must be clear, accurate, and as brief as possible. Students are often not comfortable with this kind of writing, which often contributes to their difficulty in learning science. Teachers sometimes unconsciously compare students' writing to that of scientists. The style that is expected is beyond the experience of students. If students are not meeting teachers' expectations about writing, time should be provided to help students learn the format.

Keys, Hand, Prain, and Collins (1999) propose a Science Writing Heuristic (SWH) designed to help students use written work to support their development of science understandings. They propose a template that requires students to write during the processes of their activity. Their research suggests that using the SWH supports students' metacognitive process as they make connections between procedures, data collection, evidence, and claims that they might not otherwise recognize. Students' understandings grow as they work through the heuristic to more complex concepts. The researchers conclude that by using the heuristic the students gain a better understanding of the processes and nature of scientists' work. Students are able to make connections between their science activities and their inferences, thus accomplishing the goals of science literacy as defined by the *National Science Education Standards* (NRC, 1996). Keys and her colleagues suggest that the SWH can be a bridge between traditional science writing and other genres of writing.

The SWH has two parts; the first part describes the teachers' actions and the second part includes student activities. As part of the heuristic, students answer specific questions to guide their thinking. Figure 4.8 compares the 5E Model to the SWH.

Formal Creative Writing Tasks

Scientists are creative people. Some of the greatest discoveries were made by those who "thought outside the box." Science involves both the logical and the intuitive. In Chapter 3, we mentioned the book *Cross-Pollinations* by Gary Nabhan (2004). In that book, Nabhan presents a case for creative writing by scientists. He says, " . . . fostering of creativity is essential to the advancement of science and that without it modern science will wither like an unpollinated flower . . . " (p. 44). Some students become disenfranchised if we do not encourage the creative or interpretive side of science and learning. In essence, we keep them apart from science (Hildebrand, 1998). Creative writing allows students to explore concepts and make connections to other disciplines.

> Hybrid imaginative writing includes any blended genres that use scientific and/or factual genres (recounts, procedures, reports, explanations, expositions, discussions, etc.) in conjunction with imaginative or fictional genres. (Hildebrand, 1998, p. 347)

Figure 4.8 Relationship Between the 5E Model and the Science Writing Heuristic

5E Model	Science Writing Heuristic	
	Teacher-Directed Activities	Student Writing Questions
Engage	Present a situation or example that may raise questions	

Explore	Pre-writing activities
	  Concept mapping
	  Brainstorming
	Pre-lab experiences
	  Making observations
	  Posing questions
	Informal writing
		What are my questions?

Explain	Personal reflections
	  Journal writing
	  Note taking
	Sharing data
	  Small-group work
	  Making graphs and charts
		What did I do?
		What did I find out?
		What is my claim?
		What is my evidence?

Elaborate	Compare to existing scientific knowledge Consult other sources such as textbooks, scientific journals, informational books, etc. Group writing and note taking related to questions	What do others say?

Evaluate	Individual reflections
	  Creating reports
	  Refining ideas
	  Writing explanations
	  Assessments
		How have my ideas changed?

Teachers are including creative tasks into secondary science classrooms. In Pennsylvania, Nanette Marcum-Dietrich included writing activities in her high school chemistry unit on gas laws. Her assignments included narratives, lab reports, children's books, brochures, and newspaper articles. Expectations for science content were clear. She developed rubrics used to grade the projects. Rubrics and the assignments were consistent in their emphasis on content. She also provided an opportunity for students to express their knowledge in a different way—poetry (Marcum-Dietrich, 2005). Poetry and science provide students with opportunities to gather and review ideas (Roberts, Killingsworth, & Schmidt, 2002). In the previous chapter, we referenced an article in the *Journal of Geoscience Education* that stated that poetry can support science learning. The article, "Using Poetry to Teach About Minerals in Earth Science Class," shares a teacher's experience with this form of creative writing and provides details about his lesson design (Rule et al., 2004).

Marcum-Dietrich's projects were vehicles for sharing science knowledge. Students must make decisions in order to share their knowledge in different formats to different audiences. Each project had a separate rubric to assess content knowledge while attending to formal writing conventions. Marcum-Dietrich conducted in-depth research about the processes her students used when writing in science. Her study investigated not only the science knowledge that students expressed in their writing, but also the cognitive processes that students used while writing. She found that writing activities incorporated early in the unit actually helped students form their knowledge. The activities that challenged students to use their science knowledge in new or different situations and contexts challenged students' understanding of the science content, made them think about the science content, and encouraged them to reorganize concepts (Marcum-Dietrich, 2005).

Drama is an effective means for students to express their content knowledge; students may write their own skits (Smith & Herring, 2001). In Mississippi, John Dorroh (2006) used skit writing in his high school biology class as part of his participation in the Mississippi Writing/Thinking Institute, a part of the National Writing Project. Dorroh is a coauthor of a book published by the National Science Teachers Association, *How to Write to Learn Science* (Tierney, 2004). Remember our concept web about arthropods presented in Chapter 2? The following skit was written to complement that study. Students demonstrate their understanding of arthropods—particularly insects.

The previous examples are just a few activities during which students can creatively show their content knowledge. In Chapter 3, we discussed reading science fiction and fantasy to extend content knowledge. If students have had the opportunity to analyze or criticize the work of others, they may be inspired to try the genre on their own. Many adolescents have tried to write stories on their own or they can remember writing stories in their language arts classes. Writing activities may be suggested by materials read in class. A creative writer could make a portfolio of science fiction stories throughout a yearlong course.

The list in Figure 4.10 is only the beginning. At the beginning of this chapter, we suggested that you start a writer's notebook of your own. As you find other ideas in professional journals or learn of them from colleagues, make your own list.

Figure 4.9   A Sample Skit

Creature Who?

(Scene opens with a detective and a doctor standing with a creature sitting in a chair between them.)

Detective: Doctor, we found this dark brown creature last night coming out from under a rock and he says he doesn't know who he is.

Doctor: Hmmm. Let's examine him. *(Looks at creature)* Quite interesting. His skeleton is on the outside. He has three parts to his body. Creature, stick out your legs.

Creature: Which ones? I have six you know. These long back legs like to move.

Doctor: Detective, would you please take some notes for me? Put down – outside skeleton, three body parts, six jointed legs, long back legs.

Creature: I'm awfully hungry. Do you have any seeds or old plants lying around?

Detective: We'll get to that later.

Doctor: Help me measure him, Detective. *(Takes out a ruler)* Yes, he is about one inch long. Put that in your notes. He has some wings – would you stick out your wings?

Creature: OK, but I don't use them much.

Doctor: The outside wings are rather straight.

Detective: What, wings and you don't fly much!

Creature: I'd rather hop. Listen . . . my antennae are hearing something! That rat!!! He's calling my girlfriend.

Doctor: I think I know your family name . . . does Gryllidae sound familiar?

Detective: Hey, I've heard of that family. They live down by the meadow. I love to go there in the spring and listen to them chirping. I've got it. You are a cricket.

Creature: It's coming back to me now. Thank you. I'll bring you good luck!

Figure 4.10   Creative Writing Project Ideas

- A script of an interview with a scientist who made a major discovery
- A book review of a science-related book
- A "you are there" story about a scientific event
- A diary or journal of a scientist
- An analysis of the science behind an urban legend or myth
- A review of a children's book evaluating science accuracy
- A classified ad or advertising brochure for a product
- A collection of science jokes with their explanations
- An analysis of the science (or science mistakes) in a TV show or movie
- A story set in the future showing scientific advances
- A collection of poetry showing knowledge of science concepts (see Rule et al., 2004).

ASSESSING STUDENTS' WORK

The term *assessment* may have different meanings. To some, it is a term equivalent to grading. Instead, let's use two different terms: *assessment* and *evaluation*. Assessment is collecting data (quizzes, projects, etc.). Assessment shows students' progress toward a goal. Evaluation is how you used the data; evaluation measures students' progress toward a standard. Assessments early in a unit can inform about students' progress; informal writing can provide informal assessments. At the beginning of a unit, we may not want to grade students' work; instead, we use the assessments to inform us about the types of support students may need or what kinds of resources we may need to use to help students in their inquiry. As the unit progresses, assessments may become more formal. As mentioned in the examples above, Marcum-Dietrich's (2005) research suggests that writing done early in the unit helps students form their knowledge. These assessments thus indicate students' progress toward objectives. Writing assignments at the end of a unit provide a more summative picture of what students have learned. Thus, they evaluate students' achievement of objectives.

After you have decided on a writing project, a hurdle may be deciding how to evaluate students' writing in the content areas. You may be thinking, "I'm a science teacher, not an English teacher." This is true. An approach to evaluation can be used which presents a balance between content and writing. A rubric identifies what will be evaluated and how it will be assessed.

Assessment and evaluation tasks need to be directly related to the objectives of the unit of teaching. Identify what skills and knowledge students will achieve as the result of the unit. Be specific. From this list, assessment tasks can be developed. Criteria for determining whether students have met the objective are developed next. In other words, how will you determine whether students know the content? What will you observe in their writing? These criteria should be clear and measurable.

After the criteria have been established, consider the levels of success you may see in a product. Describe what an exemplary example would look like. That description could be the highest level on your evaluation tool. Then describe what would be unacceptable; that is the lowest level of your evaluation tool. Your tool may describe several levels of success; unacceptable, satisfactory, good, or exceptional are examples of how you may describe the levels. If a project will be evaluated using a rubric that is scored by points, explain to students how points are earned.

Craft the descriptions of the levels in terms that students can understand. Explaining the criteria to students at the beginning of the project will provide students with clear expectations; they can compare their work to the criteria before the project is submitted. Encouraging students to participate in the development of a rubric encourages students to identify qualities of good projects; they learn to evaluate, a high-order task. This activity involves collaboration and consensus building consistent with social construction of knowledge. Also, students tend to take more pride and ownership in a project when they are involved in all aspects of the project. Evaluation can be an integral part of instruction.

Some states have writing assessments attached to their standards. For instance, the Pennsylvania Department of Education has developed writing rubrics to use in conjunction with persuasive, informational, and creative writing assessments. Within these rubrics, they have established five domains: focus, content, organization, style, and conventions. The domain of focus is related to students' attention to task and ability of students to make clear assertions. Content refers to the students' accurate use of details, explanations, and such that support the main idea. Organization relates to just that—does the writing have an organizational pattern that presents content logically? Style refers to the student's voice and tone that is appropriate to a specific audience. Finally, conventions relates to a student's use of spelling, grammar, punctuation, and sentence structure. These criteria are used to assess writing across all disciplines (Pennsylvania Department of Education, 2005).

More information about designing rubrics for science can be found in *Assessing Student Understanding in Science* by Sandra K. Enger and Robert E. Yeager (2001). Although this text does not specifically address writing rubrics, it does give a good description of how rubrics can be constructed for the six domains of science identified by the American Association for the Advancement of Science during the 1990s.

Whether the teacher designs a unique rubric, uses an assessment designed with students, or uses an assessment tool designed by others, the importance of science content knowledge is vital to an effective tool. Writing tasks can provide information about students' development of science concepts over time; they can give insight into students' thought processes, their misconceptions, and their ability to synthesize information.

CREATING THE ENVIRONMENT

In Chapter 3, we included a list of tips for a literacy-rich environment. Number 10 on that list suggested that opportunities for writing should be included. As we have suggested, there are many ways to include writing that range from informal to formal projects. Projects are just part of the equation. Earlier in this chapter, we discussed students who may be hesitant to write. Students who are English language learners may have additional concerns. Students who have disabilities that influence their writing may need specialized support. Creating an environment to support writing is another piece of the equation.

Students bring multiple perspectives to their science classrooms. They have different talents, interests, and prior knowledge of science concepts. An environment that respects writing as a communication tool may meet the needs of students in any classroom setting. This respectful environment will provide opportunities for students to practice writing, share their writing, and get constructive feedback about their writing. They will observe that different forms of writing can be used to convey their science knowledge.

In an inquiry-based classroom where risk taking in the form of developing questions or hypotheses is the norm, providing a safe environment for writing is also essential. Inquiry in science encourages students to be creative in their development of possibilities for data collection and research; writing is another form of creative expression. Explicit teaching of writing has been shown to increase content knowledge and the ability to effectively communicate the knowledge (Klein, 2006). Thus, in a climate where students feel safe to write, clear expectations for their writing have been explained and modeled and students have opportunities to write informally prior to formal writing. In such an environment, students are encouraged to move beyond processes and conclusions; they synthesize information to create new ideas and products. When they write, they are using higher-order cognitive processes.

Bob Tierney (2004) suggests that writing be started the first week of the semester. He begins by having students write about their own names and share the information at their lab tables. He models the strategy by reading his own essay. The second day, he has students make a sketch of the science room and write a description of the room and express their feelings about what they see. This, he explains, helps students become observers. Another day during the first week, he has students write their autobiographies of science, reflecting on their lives in terms of scientific passions they have had, how they felt about science through their school careers, and so forth. To assist students with this task, the teacher could share articles published by classroom teachers from *The American Biology Teacher* or *Journal of Geoscience Education.* The teacher writes and reads to the class again. The following day, he has students write about why they believe they need to take science. Follow-up activities based on the assignments allow students to learn to write to specific points and arguments (Tierney, 2004). His suggestions encourage teachers to interact with students, students to interact with other students, and student self-reflection.

It is important for teachers to model writing techniques for their students. Teachers should be completing writing tasks along with their students.

Students may be willing to take risks in classrooms where positive relationships have been developed. Relationships between students and between teacher and students that are positive and supportive encourage students to take risks. Students can sense an environment that encourages written communication by the attitudes and actions of those around them. Teachers can model the supportive environment by the activities that are designed and the way they respond to written work. Environments that support inquiry and environments that support writing go hand-in-hand.

SUMMARY

Writing-to-learn projects are being used more than ever before in high school science. This increase is due in part to the increasing amount of research that suggests that students benefit from the activities. Writing projects fit well into the *National Science Education Standards* (NRC, 1996) for science education because they link science to other content areas, they help students organize and clarify their science knowledge, and they are means for students to communicate their science knowledge to others.

Reading and writing support students' development of their science literacy; they complement and support science literacy. In previous chapters, we have described inquiry-based science instruction and strategies for reading to meet science content needs and needs of students. Writing activities fit well into this constructivist environment by providing opportunities for social construction of knowledge and sharing that knowledge with others. Writing tasks can range from informal to formal; they can be designed to meet students' interests and abilities while meeting science content standards. In the next chapter, we will establish a link between reading, writing, and technology in the context of inquiry-based science.

5

Using Technology to Enhance Reading, Writing, and Inquiry

Imagine that at the beginning of the year, your principal tells you that all paper and pencil supplies have been lost in shipment and there are none for your science classroom. You still need to meet the science standards. You must engage students in science discussions and discoveries; they must have opportunities to explore concepts and then explain their understandings; they must verify their results and then evaluate their conclusions. Additionally, they must be able to communicate their understandings to varied audiences. You could spend a good deal of your money at the local office supply store, but you are a problem solver and you sit down to ponder your options. Make a list of the writing tasks your students complete throughout the year—take notes, answer quizzes, record data, complete lab reports, take tests, make and label diagrams, and do research reports. Modern technology may help solve your problem.

When you hear the word *blackberry* what do you picture? Just a few years ago, you may have thought of pies. Now, talk show hosts and newscasters say they can't go anywhere without their little electronic gizmos; teenagers look at adults incredulously when adults ask how iPods work. Global positioning systems (GPSs) in our cars give us directions as we drive down the highway; TiVo records a television program while something else is on the screen or even when the owner is on vacation. Technology has certainly come a long way since one lonely computer sat in the back of a classroom waiting for the teacher to write BASIC programs because software hadn't yet been designed to use in classrooms. Sometimes new gadgets are frustrating; sometimes we yearn for the good old days. Technology is everywhere we look and some of our students may not remember a life without cell phones or the Internet.

In his book *Oversold and Underused*, Larry Cuban (2001) reports that less than 5% of teachers use technology regularly in their curriculum although most schools report having technology available. A question arises, though, about the appropriateness of the use of computers when they are actually used (Bell & Garofalo, 2005). Computers are important; nevertheless, technology appropriate for the classroom includes video, data collection devices, and other tools. We often speak of multimedia—using multiple forms of technology to meet our goals.

The National Educational Technology Standards (NETS) were developed by the International Society for Technology in Education (ISTE; 2002). The standards were developed to provide guidance for the appropriate use of technology in classrooms. Those who wish more details about ISTE and NETS may wish to investigate their publications. ISTE has published a volume which may be of interest—*National Educational Technology Standards for Students: Science Units for Grades 9–12* (Bell & Garofalo, 2005). ISTE standards center around six categories, as shown in Figure 5.1.

Figure 5.1 National Educational Technology Standards: The Next Generation

"What students should know and be able to do to learn effectively and live productively in an increasingly digital world . . . "

1. Creativity and Innovation—Students demonstrate creative thinking, construct knowledge, and develop innovative products and processes using technology.

2. Communication and Collaboration—Students use digital media and environments to communicate and work collaboratively, including at a distance, to support individual learning and contribute to the learning of others.

3. Research and Information Fluency—Students apply digital tools to gather, evaluate, and use information.

4. Critical Thinking, Problem-Solving & Decision-Making—Students use critical thinking skills to plan and conduct research, manage projects, solve problems and make informed decisions using appropriate digital tools and resources.

5. Digital Citizenship—Students understand human, cultural, and societal issues related to technology and practice legal and ethical behavior.

6. Technology Operations and Concepts—Students demonstrate a sound understanding of technology concepts, systems, and operations.

USING **85**
TECHNOLOGY
TO ENHANCE
READING,
WRITING, AND
INQUIRY

We will connect ISTE standards to inquiry and literacy in science. Standards 1 and 2 are clearly related to literacy ideas we have discussed thus far. Trying to create a balance between science content and technology can be frustrating (Tatar & Robinson, 2003), but if learning opportunities are well designed, the balance can be achieved. Standards 3 and 4 certainly have their place in the 5E Model, which encourages the incorporation of higher-order thinking skills. Standard 5 is consistent with the Science, Technology, and Society movement.

It is difficult to keep up-to-date with all the new technologies, and often our students know more about the latest tools than we do. We will look at the issue in a broad sense; we will consider learning about technology and learning to use technology. In a constructivist classroom, we learn with our students and together we can achieve Standard 6.

WHY USE TECHNOLOGY?

To be specific, we need to consider what the role of technology is in science education and what skills are necessary for science literacy. In the 1970s, a curriculum movement, Science, Technology, and Society (STS), began to identify relationships between science and technology. The goal was to have students connect technology and science knowledge in their lives and to prepare them to use that knowledge in the future (Cajas, 2001). In Chapter 1, we discussed issues related to science instruction in detail, so we will not discuss these details here. However, readers may wish to refer to the chapter as ideas are presented.

In the 1990s, STS flourished. It is difficult to get away from science and technology in contemporary society. For instance, political divisions have occurred as the result of stem-cell research over the last several years. Cloning has been accomplished in animals; is human cloning possible and, even more, is it ethical? In Chapter 3, we introduced the topic of cloning when we suggested the book, *House of the Scorpion,* by Nancy Farmer (2002). Adolescents are often interested in issues beyond themselves (Save the Whales, for instance). Bringing in issues about how technology impacts their lives and problems that may arise because of technology enhances this understanding of technology and should not be overlooked.

There are two overarching reasons to use technology: to increase student learning and to increase teacher productivity. In this chapter, we will focus on technology to increase student learning, although teacher productivity will be an added bonus. With the proliferation of video games, Web search engines, and instant messages, many students have come to expect the same experiences in classrooms. Students may not be used to reading books as we envision them; some people fear that e-books will take the place of paper books. Students' concepts of writing are influenced by blogging or e-mail. In previous chapters, we provided rationale and activities for including reading and writing in an inquiry-based classroom. Technology can provide a bridge between students' lived experiences and reading, writing, and inquiry. For instance, word processing may facilitate writing better than paper and pencil (Roberts et al., 2002).

Technology can be an asset when used effectively to enhance students' understanding of science—when the use of technology emphasizes and supports process skills and students become knowledgeable about how scientists use technology. Technology should not be used to undermine the development of scientific understanding; instead technology enhances the understanding (Bell & Garofalo, 2005). Technology in this context is an instructional tool, just one of many that can be used.

As educators, we can keep abreast of technology that is pertinent to our fields of science through professional development and professional organizations. Students may have more knowledge of some forms of technology than does the teacher. That's okay. Our role as teachers is to bridge the gap between technology that is in students' lives and technology specific to science. Sometimes, students believe that they know how to use technology but they have only a limited idea of the possibilities. For instance, students may know the mechanics of PowerPoint but do not know how to use the program to effectively communicate ideas to an audience. Students regularly search the Web, but may not know how to do so efficiently or to evaluate the quality of their search results.

When students bring their knowledge to class, teachers can model constructivist learning by allowing students to share their skills with technology. It may become overwhelming to integrate technology, especially if your science curriculum is facing many changes. It may be that you are being encouraged to use new science equipment such as new probeware, video microscopes, and graphing and statistics programs. Each of these sophisticated technologies requires time to learn and then time to decide how to use them in the classroom. A student-centered, inquiry-based environment may help (Greenberg, Raphael, Keller, & Tobias, 1998).

GETTING STARTED

Recently, a technology specialist for a local school district mentioned that he was frustrated that so many teachers were not using the computers that were in their classrooms. He lamented that it was December and one teacher hadn't even plugged in the computers. We talked for a while and came to the conclusion that sometimes the teachers just didn't know where to start. They thought they had to be experts immediately so they avoided the unknown.

Start with the students. Find out what they already know and are able to do. Identify students who have some special skills and knowledge that they can share with you and their classmates. Talk to your colleagues and friends. There may be others who have similar interests and would like to be co-learners. Internet teacher chat groups and forums provide sources for lesson plans and activities with opportunities for discussions with other teachers (Barowy & Laserna, 1997). Check professional journals and attend conferences. Check out some of the references cited in this book. Many of the Web sites for programs that we discuss have tutorials that can provide instruction and ideas for using the programs. Enjoy. Start small. Choose one type of

USING **87**
TECHNOLOGY
TO ENHANCE
READING,
WRITING, AND
INQUIRY

technology that can easily be added to your existing curriculum. After you become more comfortable, add others.

When you find a technology you would like to integrate in your class, allow students to become familiar with programs that may be new to them before they must use the programs for study. When students are trying to learn the programs while learning new content, the activity may become overwhelming and unnecessarily difficult. Allowing students to become familiar with programs in low-stress activities may take some time initially during class work. However, the benefits may outweigh the time used because the student will not need to divide learning attention to two activities simultaneously; they will be able to focus on content learning and may have a more positive experience (Grabe & Grabe, 2007).

Word processing is probably the easiest to integrate into classroom work. Writing tasks involving pencil and paper can be time consuming and messy. Editing and revising involves using multiple pages of work, drawing arrows, and crossing out. Word processing can save time and work. Students may save their work to files and disks. Go back to the literacy strategies presented in Chapters 2, 3, and 4 that require written work. Students could keep their vocabulary, reading guides, and learning logs on disks—no need for paper and pencil. Teachers will not need to struggle over reading handwriting that is almost illegible. Spelling and grammar checks may actually help students with their writing. Some studies suggest that word processing does improve writing skills and motivation to write (Grabe & Grabe, 2007).

Hypermedia

As mentioned in the previous section, limiting student use of computers as add-ons to teacher-centered instruction does not utilize technology to its fullest potential in a classroom that promotes student self-direction and inquiry. Many of these aspects can be combined through *hypermedia* programs. Hypermedia refers to software designed for organizing and managing information; the programs facilitate communication. Projects created by students may not only demonstrate several ISTE standards, but may also demonstrate understandings of science in society and science content knowledge. An example of a hypermedia program is HyperStudio, published by Sunburst Technologies. Hypermedia combines multimedia including written texts, photos, video, graphics, and sound. Hypermedia programs provide connections so that users can access individual sets of information (pages) in different orders. The information is linked like a stack of cards that can be shuffled and reordered or combined in different ways. Sets of information are cross-linked through the use of tabs or buttons. Hypermedia programs allow students to collaborate as they organize their information and design ways to share the information (Counts, 2004; Grabe & Grabe, 2007). Although hypermedia programs facilitate these activities, they are not the only way to approach technology in the classroom.

Think back to the arthropods lessons mentioned in Chapter 2. Students created a concept web prior to studying arthropods, and later, they learned related vocabulary. Later, they read sections about different kinds of arthropods using the jigsaw activity. Chapter 4 discussed the importance of communicating what students are learning and suggested writing activities. Hypermedia programs could allow students to file photos of the arthropods, create data files about different kinds of arthropods, and compose reports in an organized format.

Geocaching

Geocaching has become a popular hobby and sport with adults, and many families enjoy the activity. It is an example of a new technology that can be integrated into inquiry-based science. This activity began its popularity in 2000, when the government made GPS technology available to the general public. In May 2000, a computer consultant in Oregon, Dave Ulmer, started the rage. News of the idea spread rapidly over the Internet and the activity has become a worldwide phenomenon. *Geo* in geocaching means having to do with the earth, such as in geology or geography. *Caching* comes from French and means a storage place where things can be hidden temporarily. Another meaning of cache is related to technology—a memory cache where images are stored (Groundspeak, 2006).

In the geocaching activity, small ideas or clues are hidden and others search for the hidden objects using hints that utilize GPS technology. When searchers find items, they record their finds and leave something for the next searchers (Groundspeak, 2006; Grabe & Grabe, 2007). GPSs tell locations based upon latitude and longitude. The system recognizes the players' starting position and then provides directions to another specified location. Students could use this activity to become familiar with using GPS before they use them to collect data in an inquiry such as field study investigations. The students could have fun while they are learning new technology and new scientific vocabulary.

In an Earth Science class, a goal may be to have students learn about land formations and particularly those of the local area. Take students to a nearby state park and provide them with a geocaching activity. At each location, students could be asked to make specific observations and record their data and perhaps take photos. They could also be required to formulate questions based upon their observations. When they return to the classroom, data could be organized in a hypermedia program and used for other inquiry purposes.

USING THE INTERNET

The Internet is not really that old. In the early 1990s, educators were just beginning to see the potential. At that time, Web searching browsers were in their infancy and it was difficult to find information. When search engines became more sophisticated and easier to navigate, the use of the Internet exploded in educational circles. Most of those who use the Internet realize its value but do not really know how it works. Some think that there is a central place where the information is stored. Users often think that the information is more up-to-date than found in books (Bos, 2001; Fidel et al., 1999).

The Internet is constantly changing. Internet2 expands the capabilities of the Internet even more. Internet2 began in 1996 and was developed by

USING **89**
TECHNOLOGY
TO ENHANCE
READING,
WRITING, AND
INQUIRY

over 200 universities in the United States in collaboration with industry and government to provide advanced technological capabilities. Part of the project is the National Internet2 K20 Initiative, which brings together schools at all levels, libraries, and museums. School districts and consortiums across the country are beginning to take advantage of the technology (http://www .internet2.edu).

One cannot assume that students know how to search the Internet. Students often lack information-seeking skills; they know how to log in to the Internet but do not know how the Internet works. Students like the Web because it is fast and easy to use; they can just type in a word and get information and do not need to use card catalogs or search shelves for books. Sometimes students do not see the use of planning ahead their research; they tend to go from one site to another, and the choice is determined by what they see on the screen. Students become frustrated when sites are slow or when sites are under construction or have been moved (Fidel et al., 1999).

Students may not know about the different search engines and just tend to use the one they first learn. Students often need help deciding what words to put into the search engine. Difficulties with spelling often hinder their searches. Students usually prefer sites with graphics rather than text. Long results pages with a large amount of information may be overwhelming to students (Fidel et al., 1999).

Students require training and support for searching effectively and efficiently. Learning new information and searching skills should not be done at the same time. Prior to having students initiate a search, brainstorming about possible search terms may be done as a class activity. Aids such as a thesaurus may help students choose different search terms (Fidel et al., 1999). Vocabulary activities as suggested in Chapter 2 may help students to identify search terms.

There is a need for students learning to evaluate the material they find on the Internet; critical-thinking skills that have been developed when having students evaluate text material may be applied to evaluating Web sites. Students may not distinguish between different kinds of sites (commercial or informational). In addition to evaluating the material, students may learn to evaluate technological aspects of Web sites. They can look at the organization of material on the site. Is the site organized in a logical and useful manner? They can also look at mechanical aspects of the site—do the buttons for links work appropriately? Do the visual representations, graphs, charts, or pictures help explain the information? Is the content accurate? Is bias present? Who sponsors the site and how often is the content updated (Bos, 2001; Sharp, 2002)?

The number of Internet sites available for teachers and students is almost endless. The links that each Web site contains may lead to other sites. It is important, however, to scrutinize the links; often, sites may contain links to material that may not be appropriate. These sites may sometimes be innocently accessed. Some schools have installed filters on the school network which may deny access to inappropriate sites; however, these filters do not always filter out inappropriate sites and may actually filter out appropriate sites that happen to contain a key word or phrase that has been coded into the filter but is used in an innocent context.

Teachers may find virtual field trips and simulation activities related to most topics for science. At the end of this chapter, a list of sites you may want to visit is included. The list was verified at the time of this publication. Be aware, however, that because the Internet is constantly changing, some sites may have been moved or links may be broken. There are many sites on the Internet that can be used to supplement science instruction and aid students in data collection and analysis. Some provide opportunities for students to communicate with students and scientists worldwide.

Many Web sites have special features to help students learn about a topic. For instance, some Web sites have annotations on the page that allow students to link to explanatory information with just a click. Terms that may be difficult for students or need clarification may be written in a different color (usually blue) that signal a link to additional information. When a student clicks on the term, an automatic link may take the student to a glossary, an encyclopedia entry, a picture or video, or other background information. In earlier chapters, we discussed the importance of building background knowledge, accessing prior knowledge, and building vocabulary. Annotations on the Web page function as a tool to do so (Wallen, Plass, & Brünken, 2005).

Webquests

Students, as mentioned earlier, are used to using the Internet but often do not have Internet searching skills or knowledge to evaluate material found on Web sites. Webquests may address the problems while connecting to students' interests. Webquests can be designed to fit the steps in the 5E Model and incorporate the Science Writing Heuristic that was discussed in Chapter 4. The term *webquest* originated in the teacher education program at San Diego State University in 1995. A professor in Educational Technology, Bernie Dodge, developed a lesson format designed to encourage higher-order thinking and inquiry by using information found on the Internet. The lesson format is adaptable to one-day or full-unit projects. The benefit of the format is that the teacher selects Internet sites that students will use; this controls the quality of the sites as teachers preview sites before they are included. This can also conserve student time because they will not need to do searches. The components of a webquest are shown in Figure 5.2. Webquests can be designed for group or individual projects. The difficulty of the content is controlled by the teacher (Sharp, 2002). An extensive Web site is maintained by the Educational Technology Department of San Diego State University and is regularly updated by Bernie Dodge. The site provides templates and instructions for designing webquests, sample webquests, forums for discussing webquests, and links to other resources. Creators of webquests have the opportunity to upload their own quests to the learning community. The Web site address may be found in the list at the end of this chapter.

USING **91**
TECHNOLOGY
TO ENHANCE
READING,
WRITING, AND
INQUIRY

Figure 5.2   Components of a Webquest

Introduction

The introduction sets the purpose of the activity. It gives background information and assigns roles to students.

Task

The task tells the students what will be done and what product will be produced as the result of the quest.

Process

The process outlines the steps that will be taken to complete the task.

Resources

The resource page provides information students may need to complete their quest or suggestions about where they can find the information. Resources may include hyperlinks, videos, books, equipment, or other items that may be needed to complete the task.

Evaluation

The section tells how the product will be evaluated. Rubrics for the product are included.

Conclusion

At this point, students have the opportunity to discuss or explain what was accomplished. They will demonstrate their knowledge through their products.

SOURCE: Adapted from Sharp, V. (2002). *Computer Education for Teachers: Integrating Technology into Classroom Teaching.* (4th ed.). Boston: McGraw-Hill.

Suppose you are teaching a biology course during which you plan to address standards related to environmental and wildlife issues. The following are samples of components you could include in a study focusing on barn owls. The components could be made attractive with photos and color using templates from a webquest Internet site or by a format designed by the teacher. The same webquest could be adapted to address different forms of wildlife. The quest fits the criteria for inquiry. Students develop their own questions and propose resources they could use. They collect information and data and propose solutions. Students communicate with their peers and their teachers during their research process. Notice that students are going to make presentations to a local organization. This brings authenticity to students' work and can be motivating. If you cannot find a local organization, students could present to elementary students or other science classes. You may choose to devote as much class time as you feel necessary depending on your students. The first time students do a webquest or participate in group work, they may need more guidance.

Figure 5.3   Barn Owl Quest

Introduction

John J. Audubon was a famous ornithologist who was also known for his paintings of birds. The mission of the Audubon Society is to conserve and restore natural ecosystems, focusing on birds, other wildlife, and their habitats for the benefit of humanity and the earth's biological diversity.

http://www.audubon.org/nas/

As part of your environmental science studies, you will be participating in a study of barn owls. You will be divided into groups of four. Each person will have a role in the quest:

- Research Coordinator—Keeps file of questions and results, keeps track of sources used, assists group members with research strategies

- Written Presentation Coordinator—Collects drafts from all members, edits written project, makes sure all members contribute to written project

- Oral Presentation Coordinator—Makes sure that all members have a role in the oral presentation, coordinates presentation practices and format

- Progress Coordinator—Schedules and moderates group meetings, makes sure that all deadlines are met, liaises with teacher

Task

In our area, BARN OWLS have been put on the endangered species list because of declining population. The local Audubon Society Chapter has asked for your assistance to address the issue.

Your task will be to develop a plan to encourage an increase in BARN OWL population. Your final product will be a presentation to the local Audubon Society at one of their monthly meetings. The product will include a written document outlining the issues and a multimedia display. The tentative date of the presentation is May 17.

Process

1. In your group, develop a list of questions about the topic that you believe should be addressed as you begin this process.

2. Group the questions into categories—one category for each member of your group.

3. Assign each member a category. This member will be in charge of monitoring progress toward answering the questions. This does not mean that the person alone must answer the questions.

4. Develop a list of resources you may need to answer your questions. Compare your list to the ones provided on the Resources page. Discuss with your teacher any additional resources you feel may be necessary.

5. Begin preliminary research individually, then reconvene as a group to discuss your findings.

6. Revisit your questions and make any additions.

7. Brainstorm ideas for your presentation—what you might need, how you will organize your group to make the presentation, etc.

8. As a group, prepare a memo to the teacher outlining your plans.

USING **93**
TECHNOLOGY
TO ENHANCE
READING,
WRITING, AND
INQUIRY

9. Your teacher will review your plan and may ask additional questions.

10. After your plan is approved, you may begin.

11. You will prepare a weekly memo for the teacher outlining your progress. You may note any questions or concerns.

12. Your teacher is available for consultation—feel free to ask.

Resources

1. The school librarian has several books on reserve for you. You must ask at the reference desk and tell the librarian that you are in my class. There are also several journals that may be helpful.

2. The following Web sites may be useful.
   The American Museum of Natural History   www.amnh.org
   U.S. Fish and Wildlife Service   www.fws.gov
   Endangered Birds Gallery   http://www.50birds.gend1.htm and
            http;//www.50birds.gend2.htm
   Ornithology.com   www.ornithology.com

3. Mr. Jones has programs available in the technology lab that may be useful for your multimedia presentation. These include PowerPoint, Visual Communicator, Claymation, and Dazzle. You may make appointments with him to learn to use these and other programs.

4. The local County Conservation District has agreed to support this project. You may visit their office at 19 Fairview Street. The office is open 9–5, M–F.

5. You may use the data storage and analysis programs loaded on our lab computers.

Evaluation

Your work as an individual will be graded in several ways.

1. Our standard group participation rubric will be completed each week. The combined scores will be 20% of your grade.
2. Your written project will be graded using the School Writing Rubric (content, focus, organization, clarity, and creativity). This is a group-produced product; it will count 20% of your individual grade.
3. Your oral presentation will be graded based upon the oral presentation rubric that we use in this class. This will count 20% of your grade.

The unit will be followed by a test that covers information gathered by your group and presented by other groups. You will also be asked to write an essay describing your participation in the project. For this reason, you should keep notes from your group meetings, copies of the written products your group creates, and listen carefully to the presentations of the other groups. This test will count for 40% of your individual grade.

Conclusion

After the presentation to the Audubon Society and the completion of all classroom activities, we will discuss the quest. Be prepared to discuss questions such as these:

     What were important things you learned about endangered species?
     What did you learn about research?
     What did you learn about working in groups?
     How could the quest be improved for next year's class?

Streaming Video

Videos and DVDs are forms of technology that a teacher may use in a classroom. However, video or DVD players may break or may not always be available because they need to be shared with other teachers. Videos and DVDs may be costly and because science is a dynamic subject in which change may occur rapidly, budget constraints may preclude updating these resources. Videos wear out or become "missing." They also require storage space and cataloging (Brown, 2004). If videos are ordered from a central or consortium library, they may need to be ordered months in advance and never seem to arrive when needed; all teachers seem to be teaching the same unit at the same time.

Streaming videos can be a solution. Streaming videos are videos on demand through the Internet. The videos are available through a source such as United Streaming. United Streaming is part of Discovery Education, thus the source has a large library of videos. Typically, a school or district gains access to the videos through an annual subscription and all teachers and students have access to the site. Some states such as Georgia and Rhode Island have provided access to all schools throughout the state. The sites provide the option to search a database for available videos. The videos can then be integrated with other media. Usually, it is possible to choose specific clips from a video. The videos can be shown on an individual computer or shown through an LCD projector. Teachers may download the videos and burn them on CDs if they wish to use them when access to the Internet is not available. Because students may also access the videos, they can do individual research or view the videos outside of class (Brown, 2004).

The Globe Program

One Internet-based program that provides varied opportunities for students is the GLOBE program, which is sponsored by NASA, the National Science Foundation, and the U.S. Department of State. When schools participate in this program, students take scientific measurements in areas such as the atmosphere, soils, and hydrology. Students report the data through the Internet site. They are able to create maps and graphs and analyze data from sites around the world. They are also able to collaborate with other students and scientists. More information can be found about this program through its Web site, http://www.globe.gov. This program could easily be integrated into the Explain and Explore sections of the 5E Model.

Project Feeder Watch

Another interactive site is Project Feeder Watch sponsored by the Cornell Lab of Ornithology and other organizations such as the National Audubon Society. As part of this project, volunteers from all walks of life and areas count the birds that appear at their feeders from November through April. The project collects data about bird populations and migrations. Although there is a small participation fee, participants receive a kit that aids in their research. In the kit are data collection materials and information about birds. Participants

USING **95**
TECHNOLOGY
TO ENHANCE
READING,
WRITING, AND
INQUIRY

also keep track of weather data and look for evidence of bird diseases. Data can be submitted over the Internet. The Internet site has excellent photos that volunteers have submitted; participants submit their own photos if they wish. The program Web site provides more information including the history and results of previous studies. The URL of the site is found in the list at the end of this chapter. This site may be a companion to the book, *The Beak of the Finch* by Jonathan Weiner (1994) or Jane Yolen's children's books, *Bird Watch: A Book of Poetry* (1990) and *Owl Moon* (1987). The barn owl webquest discussed previously could be used in a classroom in conjunction with Project Feeder Watch.

Course Management Systems

Another relatively new way for teachers to integrate technology into their teaching is by using course management systems. You may also see course managements systems called Learning Management Systems or Virtual Learning Environments. At first, commercial products like Blackboard and WebCT were used, but these had some disadvantages. They could be difficult to modify if needed to meet particular situations. Also, the cost could be prohibitive. The companies producing these two systems merged in 2005. In 1999, a free open-source program called Moodle, which can be downloaded from the Internet, became available. Anyone can download it from the Moodle site. This system was originated by Martin Dougiamas, whose research involved social constructivist pedagogy and inquiry. Moodle stands for Modular Object-Oriented Dynamic Learning Environment. Thousands of educational institutions have now adopted the system. An advantage is that it can be used by a single teacher, a school district, or an institute of higher learning. It is easy to modify and is constantly evolving because those who contribute use the system themselves and see what is needed to improve the system (Cole, 2005).

Using Moodle, teachers can create whole courses or add supplemental technology-based activities to their existing courses. Teachers may create material for which a password is needed, thus providing security. The system has many components, that including forums, chats, and workshops that could fit nicely into the 5E Model. Teachers can upload documents, link to Web sites, or post assignments. Students can write journal entries and submit assignments. Students can also collaboratively create a Web document called a wiki. The document starts with one page and then each author can create a page linked to the original front page. The term comes from the Hawaiian *wiki wiki* meaning "very fast." It is a quick way for students to develop a collaborative document (Cole, 2005).

Let's go back to our opening premise. How could Moodle help eliminate the use of paper and pencil in your science classroom? Go back to your list. Think of some of your students' notebooks. Disorganized? Cumbersome? Messy? Maybe. Students could keep their notes in a space on Moodle. You could include outlines of your notes. This would be especially helpful for students who miss class. You could have students complete quizzes online, and the results could be tabulated and recorded through your Web site. Students could store their data and complete lab reports. Your imagination limits the use.

OTHER EQUIPMENT

As we mentioned earlier, technology in the classroom goes far beyond computers. Other equipment that can be used alone or with computers only enhances learning. Earlier, we mentioned GPS devices. Digital cameras and handheld computers are expanding opportunities for students to use technology inside and outside of the confines of a classroom.

Digital Cameras

A picture is worth a thousand words . . . quite trite but true. The use of digital cameras in classrooms has increased over the last few years. This can be attributed to the decreasing costs of the cameras, the ease of use, the immediacy of the pictures, and the ability to integrate the pictures with other technology. Students are able to record information, extend their knowledge, and communicate their results. By using a camera during a laboratory experience, students can record their investigative process. The cameras can increase student motivation and encourage collaboration and discussion. After their laboratory experiences, students can refer to the digital pictures to recall their processes, and the pictures can be the catalyst for discussions or written responses (Tatar & Robinson, 2003). Think back to some of the ideas we have already presented in this chapter. We suggested that students could take pictures during their geocaching field trip. If students are participating in Project Feeder Watch, they could take pictures along with keeping their logs. Digital pictures can be included as part of their presentations for their barn owl webquest. Think about ideas presented in Chapter 4. Digital pictures could serve as illustrations for creative writing activities such as poetry or children's books; they could accompany text in informational pieces. Digital pictures could serve as concrete or visual reinforcement for vocabulary and concept development.

Handheld Computers

Handheld computers have added a new dimension to technology in the classroom. They have grown from the personal digital assistants (PDAs) on which users kept appointments, phone numbers, or addresses to computers that can perform almost the same functions as a large desktop device. The capability for computing to be mobile has added to its applicability to science instruction; students and teachers can take powerful computing wherever they go. Input and output devices that can be added to the small computers increase their usability. Students can gather data and input their results anywhere—on field trips, at environmental sites, or as they work at their lab tables. The multimedia capabilities of handhelds are growing dramatically. Wireless technology has enabled students and teachers to connect to each other and other technological devices (Fascimpaur, 2003).

Many companies make handheld computers, and handhelds are compatible with both Windows and Macintosh operating systems. Those seeking handheld computers may want to look at Palm and PocketPC programs. The devices come with built-in software and software that can be installed on the user's

USING **97**
TECHNOLOGY
TO ENHANCE
READING,
WRITING, AND
INQUIRY

desktop computer so that data collected on the handheld can be communicated to the desktop by synchronizing through a USB (Universal Serial Bus) or serial connection. Handhelds also use infrared technology to beam information from one infrared device to another such as a printer, another handheld device, or a desktop computer (Fascimpaur, 2003).

Educational applications are many. Teachers can use them to collect evaluation and assessment data about students from anywhere in the classroom and then beam the information to their desktop computer. Students can take and store digital photographs for projects; they can make spreadsheets; they can gather data. Peripherals such as GPS devices, temperature and other data probes, or folding keyboards expand the uses of handhelds. Students can compose parts of a written report individually and then beam their work to others in their group. Creative teachers and students find many uses for handhelds (Fascimpaur, 2003).

DATA ANALYSIS PROGRAMS

As students become involved in active learning, they are encouraged to collect and analyze data. Often, the data storage, retrieval, and manipulation takes valuable time and detracts from concept development and understanding because students become overwhelmed with data. Vernier's Graphical Analysis program has been used in classrooms for many years. It was originally designed for Apple computers but has now been upgraded to be used with Windows programs. It is also compatible with many Texas Instrument calculators. Some additional benefits of this program are that it is inexpensive and easy to use. It will also accept data from some handheld computers. Students can copy and paste data from other programs such as Microsoft Excel or import data from a text file. The versatile program creates and prints graphs and data tables, performs automatic curve fits, and calculates statistics, tangents, interpolations, and integrals. Vernier also makes a portable data collection and entry device (LabPro) that can be used in and out of the classroom from which data can be uploaded to the graphical analysis program.

Databases

Databases provide means to organize information that has been collected about a topic. For instance, a teacher could create an inventory of science equipment and supplies used during a school year. The amount of supplies on hand could be entered and updated as the supplies are used. The database could also include information about the units or lessons that use the supplies, storage requirements for particular supplies, or even catalogs or companies from which the supplies are usually ordered. Then when budget time comes, the information could be retrieved to make ordering quicker and easier.

There are four major terms associated with databases: *file, record, field*, and *report*. The file is the name of the collection or topic. Consider this to be a large, accordion-type file folder. This is the folder where all material related to the topic will be kept. The record can be compared to a single file folder which will be kept in the accordion file. This is information connected to a subtopic. The field identifies the specific type of information in the record. The report is a document created to show specific fields of the data.

Let's consider a database created on Microsoft Access, which is a fairly easy-to-use program. If students are studying owls, they may be required to keep information about the owls' habitats, food, mating, size, range, distinguishing characteristics, and scientific names. They could keep the information in notebooks or on file cards. However, if they want to compile specific information, they would need to search through their written materials and copy the information they needed. A database program will make their work easier and faster.

Spreadsheets

Spreadsheets are similar to databases in that they are tools to store and organize information. However, spreadsheets are more appropriate for quantitative data. Many programs have the capability to create graphs and charts from the information. One popular program is Microsoft Excel. Terms associated with spreadsheets are *workbooks, sheets, rows, cells,* and *functions.* The workbook is the file; this could be compared to an account book for a particular project. The sheets are the pages in the file where data is recorded. Rows are horizontal and are labeled with numbers. Columns are vertical and are labeled with letters. Cells are the spaces where the rows and columns intersect and are labeled with a letter and a number. For instance, the cell in the third column and fifth row would be cell C5. The type of data that can be put in each cell includes texts, numbers, and formulas. If students were keeping track of information gathered in a physics experiment related to time, distance, and rate, they could enter a trial number at the beginning of each row. The columns could be labeled distance, rate, and time. The spaces where the rows and columns intersect are the cells in which students could enter the numerical data gathered from their trials. Formulas could be inserted in the cells so that unknown quantities could be calculated when other variables are known.

Most spreadsheets are programmed to do mathematical operations—addition, subtraction, multiplication, and division. They are also able to do mathematical functions such as finding average, maximum values, minimum values, counts, and if statements. The spreadsheets will also do calculations to find sine, cosine, and tangents. Cells that contain equations or formulas automatically do calculations using data entered into the spreadsheet. Users can generate different kinds of graphs such as bar graphs or circle graphs from the data in the spreadsheet. The spreadsheets help students organize and analyze their data. This technology can aid students by making their calculations faster and easier so that they can "get down to business" and understand science concepts without being frustrated with mathematical calculations and constructing time-consuming graphs when the lesson objective is to analyze data.

USING **99**
TECHNOLOGY
TO ENHANCE
READING,
WRITING, AND
INQUIRY

TECHNOLOGY AND WRITING

In Chapter 4 we discussed writing as a method for expressing science knowledge. Technology can support writing from the pre-writing to the publishing stage. Databases can provide sources of information for writing. Programs such as Filemaker Pro allow students to sort and organize their information. Many of these tools are technological equivalents of a writer's notebook like the one suggested in Chapter 4. Multimedia tools such as HyperStudio or PowerPoint can be used to publish their information.

After students have had the opportunity to explore topics and collect and analyze data to make decisions, they are ready to communicate their findings. Often, they are asked to make formal written presentations of information. If we were to create a webquest about barn owls, students may be asked to create a document to present at an Audubon Society meeting. There are several quality programs available to aid students in this step. In this case, we will refer to Microsoft Publisher. The program provides templates and style sheets to guide students in their project. The program, like many word processing programs, provides aids such as a spell checker and a grammar checker. Students may also add graphics to make their product more interesting. In the barn owl example, students could create a brochure about barn owls that would include information required by the task on the webquest or create a newsletter about their progress with the project.

Inspiration

Inspiration is a program that is applicable to writing activities, but it can also be used to support inquiry projects—both activities involve brainstorming and organizing ideas. The program includes formats for students and teachers to create concept webs and other graphic organizers to support students. If we think back to the 5E Model, students are encouraged to do concept mapping and brainstorming in the Exploration step. The information on the concept web can be easily transformed into a formal outline with the program. Teachers can use the program to create blank concept webs or templates for students to enter data or students may create their own. The concept webs can be saved as files and later imported into documents or Web pages with hyperlinks.

Claymation

Animated movies are becoming more sophisticated and popular as entertainment. Art and science combine to understand how animation works. Movies are actually made of a series of still frames shown at a high speed that fool the eye into thinking the figures are moving. Claymation is a program that combines clay, digital photography, and video production using a computer. To create a video, users form figures from clay, then take digital pictures, and combine these pictures into a video. Students can use the program to explain their scientific knowledge. Consider, for example, students are presenting their understanding of simple machines. How many times have students been asked to draw diagrams explaining how the machines work? Instead, students could make animated figures to demonstrate pulleys, levers, wheels and axles, screws, and inclined planes. Students must first write a script and then produce the video, thus combining writing skills and scientific knowledge with different frames demonstrating different concepts. For instance, the clay characters could be presented with the fulcrums of a lever placed in different positions relative to what is being lifted. Students could supplement the visuals with sound effects. This may take a little more time than drawing the diagrams, but for some students the act of creating the project may provide the repetition and reinforcement necessary to understand and apply the concepts. More advanced students could present the equations for leverage, and students interested in technology could have opportunities to explore their interests.

Visual Communicator

Visual Communicator is a program that allows users to create presentations or video productions easily. Students can share their information as newscasts or other video documentaries. The program wizard guides users through the creation of their product. Users can import videos, PowerPoint slides, still pictures, or information from other devices. The imported items can be combined with material recorded on a camcorder or video camera in front of a green screen to give the product a professional look. Sound can also be added as well as graphics. Imagine that students who completed research about barn owls as suggested earlier in this chapter shared their information in a documentary video. Students would learn the planning and production process. The experience could be expanded into an STS activity during which students would consider the impact that television and movies have upon environmental issues. They could discuss the role that former vice president Al Gore's movie, *An Inconvenient Truth* (2005), had on public opinion.

EVALUATING SOFTWARE PROGRAMS

With so many programs available, the task of choosing programs to use in one's classroom can be daunting. If we support the premise that our primary goal is to have students learn science, then we must match the technology to the goal. A seamless connection should be made between the two; the focus should not be on the technology but the science. The first question to be asked is "What is the objective of the inquiry?" As science teachers who are supporting inquiry-based, constructivist learning, we may find that some programs that focus on behaviorism and teacher-directed learning may not be consistent with our theoretical perspectives. Vicki Sharp (2002) suggests the following criteria:

- Does the program have a theoretical base consistent with curricular objectives?
- Does the program match the knowledge and skills of the students?
- How accurate is the information in the program (content, grammar, etc.)?
- How much time is needed to run the program?
- Is the program free of stereotypes or biases?

USING **101**
TECHNOLOGY
TO ENHANCE
READING,
WRITING, AND
INQUIRY

- Is there flexibility in the program? Can students move back and forth and control the speed of the program? Is it adaptable for different levels?
- What kind of reinforcement is provided in the program, and is the feedback motivating?
- Is the instructional sequence appropriate?
- Can the program be adapted to individual, small-, or large-group instruction?
- Does the program provide information about the students' progress?
- Is the program visually appealing?
- Are the instructions clear and easy to follow?
- Is the program easy to learn?
- How does the cost compare to the benefit?
- What kinds of technical support are available?

CHALLENGES

Using technology in a classroom can aid students, but technology use can also present challenges. There are many devices that can be used, but students may not have access to the equipment. Students' access to technology that can be used for adaptations can be limited by educational, economic, attitudinal, or cultural influences. Physical limitations may hinder students' use of computers. Students may be color blind, blind or partially blind, or unable to read small text and may have trouble when they are asked to use the Internet. Screen magnifiers can be used to aid those who have some sight. Alternate browsing methods are available such as Braillesurf, which allows the information to be read on a Braille bar or a speech synthesizer. Text-to-speech or screen-reading utilities are available, and speech recognition software provides computer dictation and composition options for students with the cognitive ability to understand the technology (Williamson, Wright, Schauder, & Bow, 2001). For those who have physical disabilities that limit their manual dexterity, a specialized mouse or specialized keyboards for their range of motion, or even eye-gaze systems, are available. Students who are nonverbal can communicate in and out of their classrooms using a variety of simple or sophisticated augmentative specialized software.

SUMMARY

According to some predictions, 25% of all new jobs created by 2010 will need technological skills. We may have students who for various reasons do not have access to some technologies that many of us take for granted. Access to computers and related technologies may be limited by economic and social forces such as gender or racial/ethnic differences. Teachers are challenged by this diversity. Integrating technology is not only important for success after students graduate from school, but it also important for success in school because a digital divide among students may limit some students' access to knowledge in their content areas (Cooper & Weaver, 2003).

The main role of technology is to encourage student learning—to make learning meaningful. Technology can promote active interaction with knowledge; active learning is both hands-on and minds-on and is central to science as inquiry. Authentic, challenging tasks help students make connections with science content and their lives. Tasks that are authentic may vary according to students' culture; what students learn may differ from what teachers expect or plan. Students may not be able to connect what they are learning in class in practical situations. Students may have misconceptions or ideas that are not compatible with what they are learning in school; therefore, if activities in class can utilize technology from the students' lives to help students interact with new knowledge that can be applied to their own lives, learning is enhanced (Grabe & Grabe, 2007). Specific programs and technology tools may serve functions that can fit into inquiry-based lessons and require varying levels of cognition. At the end of this chapter, we will provide sources for programs ranging from stand-alone to multimedia that have been mentioned in this chapter. The list is not all-inclusive—there are many more programs that could be used—but is intended to be a springboard for thought. Also included at the end of the chapter is a list of Internet sites mentioned in the chapter.

SOURCES FOR COMPUTER PROGRAMS REFERENCED IN THIS CHAPTER

Blackboard (www.blackboard.com)
  Blackboard Inc.
  1899 L Street NW 11th Floor
  Washington, DC 20036
Claymation (www.mediapostinc.com)
  Media Post, Inc.
  306 E. Grandview Avenue
  Zelienople, PA 16063
Filemaker Pro (www.filemaker.com)
  Filemaker, Inc.
  5201 Patrick Henry Drive
  Santa Clara, CA 95054
Hyperstudio (www.hyperstudio.com)
  Sunburst Technologies
  1550 Executive Drive
  Elgin, IL 60123
Inspiration (www.inspiration.com)
  Inspiration Software, Inc.
  9400 SW Beaverton-Hillsdale Highway
  Beaverton, OR 97005-3300
Microsoft Office (www.microsoft.com)
(including PowerPoint, Access, Excel, and Publisher)
  Microsoft Corporation
  One Microsoft Way
  Redmond, WA 98052-6399

USING **103**
TECHNOLOGY
TO ENHANCE
READING,
WRITING, AND
INQUIRY

Palm and PocketPC (www.palm.com)
    950 W. Maude Avenue
    Sunnyvale, CA 94085
RealPlayer (Presenter One) (www.realnetworks.com)
    Real Networks, Inc.
    2601 Elliott Avenue
    Seattle, WA 98121
United Streaming (www.unitedstreaming.com)
    Discovery Education
    1560 Sherman Avenue
    Suite 100
    Evanston, IL 60201
Vernier Software and Technology (www.vernier.com)
    13979 SW Milikan Way
    Beaverton, OR 97005
Visual Communicator (www.seriousmagic.com)
    101 Parkshore Drive
    Suite 250
    Folsom, CA 95630
WebCT (see Blackboard)

WEB SITES REFERENCED IN THIS CHAPTER

Globe	www.globe.gov
Groundspeak	www.groundspeak.com
Internet2	www.internet2.edu
Moodle	www.moodle.com
Project Feeder Watch	www.birds.cornell.edu/pfw
San Diego Webquests	www.webquests.sandiego.edu

ADDITIONAL WEB SITES OF INTEREST

http://www.exploratorium.com/
Exploratorium
The museum of science, art and human perception
Palace of Fine Arts, 3601 Lyon Street,
San Francisco, CA 94123

http://www.execulink.com/~ekimmel/dissect.htm
Link for online dissections

http://www.osti.gov/sciencelab/highschool.html
Government Science Site

http://www.telementor.org
Resources for inquiry-/problem-based activities

References

Aczel, A. D. (2003). *Pendulum: Léon Foucault and the triumph of science.* New York: Atria.

Airasian, P., & Walsh, M. (1997). Cautions for classroom constructivists. *Phi Delta Kappan, 78*(6), 444–449.

American Association for the Advancement of Science (AAAS). (1993). *Benchmarks for science literacy.* New York: Oxford University Press.

Barowy, B., & Laserna, C. (1997). The role of the Internet in the adoption of computer modeling as legitimate high school science. *Journal of Science Education and Technology, 9*(1), 3–13.

Battistich, V., Solomon, D., Kim, D., Watson, M., & Schaps, E. (1995). Schools as communities, poverty, levels of student populations, and students' attitudes, motives, and performances: A multilevel analysis. *American Educational Research Journal, 32*(3), 627–658.

Beebe, W. (1988). *The book of naturalists: An anthology of the best natural history.* Princeton, NJ: Princeton University Press.

Bell, R. L., & Garofalo, J. (2005). *National Educational Technology Standards for Students: Science units for grades 9–12.* Eugene, OR: International Society for Technology in Education.

Bentley, M., & Alouf, J. (2003, January). *The influence of the modeling of inquiry-based science teaching by science faculty in P–12 teacher professional development programs.* Paper presented at the annual meeting of the American Association of Colleges for Teacher Education, New Orleans, LA.

Bentley, M., Ebert, C., & Ebert, E. (2002). *The natural investigator: A constructivist approach to elementary and middle school science.* Belmont, CA: Wadsworth/Thomson Learning.

Berenson, S. B., & Carter, G. S. (1995). Changing assessment practices in science and mathematics. *School Science and Mathematics, 95*(4), 182–186.

Berlinski, D. (2000). *Newton's gift: How Sir Isaac Newton unlocked the system of the world.* New York: The Free Press.

Berman, B. (1995). *Secrets of the night sky: The most amazing things in the universe you can see with the naked eye.* New York: William Morrow.

Berman, B. (2003). *Strange universe: The weird and wild science of everyday life—On earth and beyond.* New York: Henry Holt.

Bingham, C., Morgan, B., & Robertson, M. (Eds.). (2007). *Buzz: What's all the buzz about these bugs?* New York: DK Publishing.

Bos, N. (2001). High school students' critical evaluation of scientific resources on the World Wide Web. *Journal of Science Education and Technology, 9*(2), 161–175.

Brown, K. (Ed.). (1998). *Verse and universe: Poems about science and mathematics.* Minneapolis, MN: Milkweed Edition.

Brown, L. (2004). Streaming video—The wave of the video future! *Library Media Connection, 23*(3), 54–56.

Butzow, C., & Butzow, J. (2000). *Science through children's literature: An integrated approach* (2nd ed.). Englewood, CO: Teacher Ideas Press.

Cajas, F. (2001). The science/technology interaction: Implications for science literacy. *Journal of Research in Science Education, 38*(7), 715–729.

Capra, F. (2007). *The science of Leonardo: Inside the mind of the great genius of the Renaissance.* New York: Doubleday.

Carnine, L., & Carnine, D. (2004). The interaction of reading skills and science content knowledge when teaching struggling secondary students. *Reading and Writing Quarterly, 20,* 203–218.

Carson, R. (1967). *Silent spring.* New York: Fawcett. (Original work published 1962)

Cartier, J. L., & Stewart, J. (2000). Teaching the nature of inquiry: Further developments in a high school genetics curriculum. *Science and Education, 9,* 247–264.

Caseau, D., & Norman, K. (1997). Special education teachers' use of science-technology-society (STS) themes to teach science to students with learning disabilities. *Journal of Science Teacher Education, 8*(1), 55–68.

Chamberlain, G. K. (1999). *Student perceptions of their middle school learning environment.* Unpublished doctoral dissertation, The Pennsylvania State University, University Park, PA.

Chamberlain, K. (2003). *Middle schools for a diverse society.* New York: Peter Lang.

Chesbro, R. (2006). Using interactive notebooks for inquiry-based science. *Science Scope, 29*(7), 30–34.

Chiappetta, E., & Koballa, T. (2002). *Science instruction for middle and secondary schools: Developing fundamental knowledge and skills for teaching* (6th ed.). Upper Saddle River, NJ: Prentice-Hall.

Colburn, A., & Clough, M. P. (1997). Implementing the learning cycle. *The Science Teacher, 64*(5), 30–33.

Cole, J. (2005). *Using Moodle: Teaching with the popular open source course management system.* Sebastopol, CA: O'Reilly.

Collins, A. (1986, January). *A sample dialogue based on a theory of inquiry teaching* (Technical Report No. 367). Cambridge, MA: Bolt, Beranek, and Newman.

Cooper, J., & Weaver, K. D. (2003). *Gender and computers: Understanding the digital divide.* Mahwah, NJ: Lawrence Erlbaum Assosciates.

Counts, E. L., Jr. (2004). *Multimedia design and production for students and teachers.* Boston: Pearson Education.

Crane, C. (1998). *Rural elementary teachers' perceptions of science education reform.* Unpublished doctoral dissertation, The Pennsylvania State University, University Park, PA.

Crane, C., & Chamberlin, K. (2004). Middle school students' perception of how they learn science: Support for inquiry-based science. *CESI Science, 37*(2), 20–31.

Cuban, L. (2001). *Oversold and underused: Computers in the classroom*: Cambridge, MA: Harvard University Press.

Cullinan, B., Scala, M. C., & Schroder, V. C. (1995). *Three voices: An invitation to poetry across the curriculum.* York, ME: Stenhouse.

Cummins, J., Brown, K., & Sayers, D. (2007). *Literacy, technology, and diversity: Teaching for success in changing times.* Boston: Pearson Education.

DeBoer, G. E. (1991). *A history of ideas in science education.* New York: Teachers College Press.

DeBoer, G. E. (2000). Scientific literacy: Another look at its historical and contemporary meanings and its relationship to science education reform. *Journal of Research in Science Teaching, 37,* 582–601.

Dobb. F. (2004). *Essential elements of effective science instruction for English learners* (2nd ed.). Los Angeles: California Science Project.

Dorroh, J. (2006). How enzymes act: Skit writing in science class. *The Quarterly, Fall,* 13–17.

Downing, J. L. (2005). *Teaching literacy to students with significant disabilities: Strategies for the K-12 inclusive classroom.* Thousand Oaks, CA: Corwin Press.

Driver, R., Asoko, H., Leach, J., Mortimer, E., & Scott, P. (1994). Constructing scientific knowledge in the classroom. *Educational Researcher, 23*(7), 5–12.

Eisenkraft, A. (2003). Expanding the 5E model. *The Science Teacher, 70*(6), 56–59.

Ellsworth, M. S. (2002). *Some assisted reading strategies for using science textbooks.* Retrieved June 22, 2006, from http://www.rit.edu/~comets/teachingcurrlmreadingstrategies.htm

Enger, S. K., & Yeager, R. E. (2001). *Assessing student understanding in science.* Thousand Oaks, CA: Corwin Press.

Farmer, N. (2002). *The house of the scorpion.* New York. Simon & Schuster.

Fascimpaur, K. (2003). *101 great educational uses for your handheld computer.* Long Beach, CA: K12 Handhelds.

Ferrero, D. (2005). Does research based mean value neutral? *Phi Delta Kappan, 86*(6), 425.

Fidel, R., Davies, R. K., Douglass, M. H., Holder, J. K., Hopkins, C. J., Kusher, E. J., et al. (1999). A visit to the information mall: Web searching behavior of high school students. *Journal of the American Society for Information Science, 50*(1), 24–37.

Fisher, A. (2001). *Sing of the earth and sky: Poems about our planet and the wonders beyond.* Honesdale, PA: Boyds Mills.

Fisher, L. (2002). *How to dunk a doughnut: The science of everyday life.* New York: Penguin.

Fleischman, J. (2002). *Phineas Gage: A gruesome but true story about brain science.* Boston: Houghton Mifflin.

Fletcher, R. (1996). A writer's notebook: Unlocking the writer within you. New York: HarperCollins.

Gabler, I. C., & Schroeder, M. (2003). *Constructivist methods for the secondary classroom: Engaged minds.* Boston: Allyn & Bacon.

Gaskins, I., Guthrie, J., Satlow, E., Ostertag, J., Six, L., Byrne, J., et al. (1994). Integrating instruction of science, reading, and writing: Goals, teacher development, and assessment. *Journal of Research in Science Teaching, 31*(9), 1057–1073.

Genge, N. E. (2002). *The forensic casebook: The science of crime scene investigation.* New York: Random House.

Goodnough, K. (2001). Multiple intelligences theory: A framework for personalizing science. *School Science and Mathematics, 101*(4), 180–192.

Gorman, M. & Smith, J. (2003). *Getting graphic: Using graphic novels to promote literacy with preteens and teens.* Columbus, OH: Linworth Publishing, Inc.

Grabe, M., & Grabe, C. (2007). *Integrating technology for meaningful learning* (5th ed.). Boston: Houghton Mifflin.

Greenberg, R., Raphael, J., Keller, J. L., & Tobias, S. (1998). Teaching high school science using image processing: A case study of implementation of computer technology. *Journal of Research in Science Teaching, 35*(3), 297–327.

Grossen, B., Romance, N. R., & Vitale, M. (1994). Science: Educational tools for diverse learner. *School Psychology Review, 23*(3), 442–463.

Groundspeak. (2006). *The history of geocaching.* Retrieved November 13, 2006, from http://geocaching.com/about/history.aspx

Gunel, M., Hand, B., & Gunduz, S. (2006). Comparing student understanding of quantum physics when embedding multimodal representations into two different writing formats: Presentation format versus summary report format. *Science Education, 90*, 1092–1112.

Guzzetti, B., Taylor, T. E., Glass, G. V., & Gammas, W. S. (1993). Promoting conceptual change in science: A comparative meta-analysis of instructional interventions from reading education and education. *Reading Research Quarterly, 28*, 117–159.

Hadaway, N. L., Vardell, S. M., & Young, T. A. (2002). Linking science and literature for ESL students. *Book Links, 12*(2). Retrieved May 23, 2005, from www.ala.org

Hand, B., & Prain, V. (2002). Teachers implementing writing-to-learn strategies in junior secondary science: A case study. *Science Education, 86*, 737–755.

Hand, B. M., Prain, V., Lawrence, C., & Yore, L. A. (1999). Writing in science framework designed to enhance science literacy. *International Journal of Science Education, 10*, 1021–1036.

Haury, D. (1993). *Teaching science through inquiry.* Retrieved April 15, 2008, from www.ericdigests.org/1993/inquiry.htm

Harris, N. (2004). *Exploring science and medical discoveries – cloning.* Farmington Mills, MI: Greenhaven Press.

Highfield, R. (2002). *The science of Harry Potter: How magic really works.* New York: Penguin.

Hildebrand, G. M. (1998). Disrupting hegemonic writing practices in school science: Contesting the right way to write. *Journal of Research in Science Teaching, 35*(4), 345–362.

Hohenshell, L. M., & Hand, B. (2006). Writing-to-learn strategies in secondary school cell biology: A mixed method study. *International Journal of Science Education, 28*(2–3), 261–289.

Howes, E. V., Hamilton, G. W., & Zaskoda, D. (2003). Linking science and literature through technology: Thinking about interdisciplinary inquiry in middle school. *Journal of Adolescent and Adult Literacy, 48*(8), 484–504.

Huber, R. A., & Walker, B. (2002). Helping students read textbooks. *Science Scope, 26*(4), 39–40.

International Society for Technology in Education (ISTE). (2002). *National Educational Standards for Teachers: Preparing teachers to use technology.* Eugene, OR: Author.

Jargodski, C. P., & Potter, F. (2001). *Mad about physics: Braintwisters, paradoxes, and curiosities.* New York: Wiley.

Jay, L. A. (2000). *Sea turtles.* Minnetonka, MN: Northwood.

Johnson, G. (2005). *Miss Leavitt's stars: The untold story of the woman who discovered how to measure the universe.* New York: Atlas.

Kane, S. (2007). *Integrating literature in the content areas: Enhancing adolescent learning and literacy.* Scottsdale, AZ: Holcomb Hathaway.

Karukstis, K. K., & Van Hecke, G. (2003). *Chemistry connections: The chemical basis of everyday phenomena* (2nd ed.). San Diego, CA: Academic Press.

Keys, C., Hand, B., Prain, V., & Collins, S. (1999). Using the science writing heuristic as a tool for learning from laboratory investigations in secondary science. *Journal of Research in Science Teaching, 36*, 1065–1084.

Kies, C. N. (1992). *Presenting young adult horror.* Independence, KY: Twayne Publishers.

King, K. P. (2007). *Integrating the national science education standards into classroom practice.* Upper Saddle River, NJ: Pearson-Prentice Hall.

Kjelle, M. M. (2005). *Antoine Lavoiser: Father of modern chemistry.* New York: Mitchell Lane.

Klein, P. D. (2006). The challenges of scientific literacy: From the viewpoint of a second-generation cognitive scientist. *International Journal of Science Education, 28*(2–3), 143–178.

Kluger-Bell, B. (2000). Recognizing inquiry: Comparing three hands-on teaching techniques, *Foundations Monograph Series, Volume 2, Inquiry thoughts, views, and strategies for the K–5 classroom,* 39–50. Arlington, VA: National Science Foundation.

Krauss, L. M. (1995). *The physics of Star Trek.* New York: HarperCollins.

Kulm, G., Roseman, J. E., & Treistman, M. (1999). A benchmarks-based approach to textbook evaluation. *Science Books & Films, 35*(4). Retrieved October 10, 2006, from http://www.project 2061.org/publications

Kyle, W., Bonnestetter, R., McCloskey, S., & Fults, B. (1985). What research says: Science through discovery: Students love it. *Science and Children, 23*(2), 39–41.

Lauber, P. (1986). *Volcano: The eruption and healing of Mount St. Helens.* New York: Harcourt Brace.

Lawson, A. E. (1995*). Science teaching and the development of thinking.* Belmont, CA: Wadsworth.

Lear, L. (1997). *Rachel Carson. Witness for a nation.* New York: Henry Holt.

Lewis, J. P. (2004). *Scien-trickery: Riddles in science.* New York: Harcourt.

Llewellyn, D. (2005). *Teaching high school science through inquiry: A case study approach.* Thousand Oaks, CA: Corwin Press.

Lowry, L. (1993). *The giver.* Boston: Houghton Mifflin.

Macaulay, D. (1988). *The way things work.* Boston: Houghton Mifflin.

Macaulay, D. (2000). *Building big.* Boston: Houghton Mifflin.

Manner, B. M. (2001). Learning styles and multiple intelligences in students: Getting the most out of your students' learning. *Journal of College Science Teaching, 30*(6), 390–393.

Marcum-Dietrich, N. J. (2005). Investigating the writing strategies used and content knowledge gained by secondary science students. *Dissertation Abstracts International, 66*(03) 948. (AAT No. 3169522)

Maruki, T. (1982) *Hiroshima no pika.* New York: HarperCollins.

Mass, W. (Ed.). (2001). *Children's literature.* San Diego, CA: Greenhaven.

Mastropieri, M., Leinart, A., & Scruggs, T. E. (1999). Strategies to increase reading fluency. *Intervention in School and Clinic, 34*(5), 278–283, 292.

Mastropieri, M., & Scruggs, T. (1992). Science for students with disabilities. *Review of Educational Research, 62*(4), 377–411.

Mastropieri, M., & Scruggs, T. (2001). Promoting inclusion in secondary classrooms. *Learning Disability Quarterly, 24*(4), 265–274.

Matkins, J. J., & Brigham, F. (1999, January). *A synthesis of empirically supported best practices for science students with learning disabilities.* Paper presented at the International Conferences of the Association for Educating Teachers in Science, Austin, TX.

Mattheis, F., & Nakayama, G. (1988, September). Effects of a laboratory-centered inquiry program on laboratory skills, science process skills, and understanding of science knowledge in middle grades students. (ED 307 148)

Mavity, R. (2007). Local scientist's humungous fungus verified by new study. *Cape Gazette 15*(1), Lewes, DE: Cape Gazette Limited.

Mayer, D. A. (1995). How can we best use literature in teaching? *Science and Children 32*(6), 16–44.

McGee, H. (2004). *On food and cooking: The science and lore of the kitchen.* New York: Scribner.

McKenna, M. C., & Robinson, R. D. (2006). *Teaching through text: Reading and writing in the content areas* (4th ed.). Boston: Pearson Education.

Miller, J. D. (1998). The measurement of civic scientific literacy. *Public Understanding of Science, 7,* 203–223.

Minyard, A. (1998). *Decades of science fiction.* Lincolnwood, IL: NTC.

Moussiaux, S., & Norman, J. (2005). *Constructivist teaching practices: Perceptions of teachers and students.* Retrieved June 7, 2005, from http://www.ed.psu.edu/ci/Journals/97pap32.htm

Nabhan, G. P. (2004). *Cross-pollinations: The marriage of science and poetry.* Minneapolis, MN: Milkweed Editions.

National Research Council. (1996). *National science education standards.* Washington, DC: National Academies Press.

National Research Council. (1999). *How people learn: Bridging research and practice.* Washington, DC: National Academies Press.

National Science Board. (1991). *Science & engineering indicators—1991.* Washington, DC: U.S. Government Printing Office.

National Science Teacher's Association (NSTA). (2004). Students with disabilities. An NSTA position statement. Retrieved June 10, 2008, from http://www.nsta.org/about/positions/disabilities/aspx

National Science Teachers Association (NSTA). (2005). The use and adoption of textbooks in science teaching. An NSTA background paper. Retrieved May 23, 2005, from http://www.nsta.org/textbooks

Nickelson, D. (2004). Portfolios in physics. *The Science Teacher, 71*(4), 52–55.

Nilsen, A. P., & Donelson, K. (2001). *Literature for today's young adults.* New York: Longman.

Nordstrom, V. (1992). Reducing the text burden: Using children's literature and trade books in elementary school science education. *Reference Services Review, 20*(1), 57–70.

Norris, S. P., & Phillips, L. M. (2003). How literacy in its fundamental sense is central to scientific literacy. *Science Education 87*(2), 224–240.

Osborne, M., & Freyberg, P. (1985). *Learning in science: Implications of children's knowledge.* Auckland, New Zealand: Heinemann.

Park, D.-Y. (2005). Differences between a standards-based curriculum and traditional textbooks in high school earth science. *Journal of Geoscience Education, 53*(5), 540–547.

Paulson, F. L., & Paulson, P. R. (1990, August). *How do portfolios measure up?* Paper presented at Aggregating Portfolio Data conference, Union, WA.

Pennsylvania Department of Education. (2005). *Writing assessment handbook 2005–2006.* Harrisburg, PA: Author.

Prain, V. (2006). Learning from writing is secondary science: Some theoretical and practical implications. *International Journal of Science Education, 28*(2–3), 179–201.

Prain, V., & Hand, B. (1999). Student perceptions of writing for learning in secondary school science. *Science Education, 83,* 151–162.

Preston, R. (1994). *The hot zone.* New York: Random House.

Preston, R. (1996). *First light: The search for the edge of the universe* (rev. ed.). New York: Random House.

Preston, R. (2008). *About Richard Preston.* Retrieved April 16, 2008, from http://www.richardpreston.net.

Raham, G. (2004). *Teaching science fact with science fiction.* Portsmouth, NH: Teacher Idea Press.

Rakow, S. (1998). *Teaching science as inquiry. Fastback 246.* Bloomington, IN: Phi Delta Kappa Educational Foundation.

Regan, T., Case, C., & Brubacker, J. (2000). *Understanding of scientific inquiry.* Thousand Oaks, CA: Corwin Press.

Rescher, R. (2000). *Inquiry dynamics.* New Brunswick, NJ: Transaction.

Richardson, V. (1999). Teacher education and the construction of meaning. In G. A. Griffin (Ed.), *The education of teachers: Ninety-eighth yearbook of the National Society for the Study of Education* (pp. 145–166). Chicago: University of Chicago Press.

Rivard, L. P. (2004). Are language-based activities in science effective for all students, including low achievers? *Science Education, 88*(3), 420–442.

Roberts, S. K., Killingsworth, S., & Schmidt, D. (2002). Enhancing poetry writing through technology: The yin and the yang. *Reading Horizons, 42*(3), 215–229.

Roe, B., Stoodt-Hill, B., & Burns, P. (2007). Secondary school literacy instruction: The content areas (9th ed.). Boston: Houghton Mifflin.

Roseman, J. L., Kesidou, S., & Stern, L. (1997). *Identifying curriculum materials for science literacy: A project 2061 evaluation tool.* Retrieved October 10, 2006, from http://www.project2061.org/publications

Rosenblatt, L. M. (1991). Literature—S. O. S.! *Language Arts, 68,* 444–448.

Roth, W. M. (1992). Dynamic evaluation. *Science Scope, 15*(6), 37–40.

Rubin, C. S., & Wilson, S. (2001). Inquiry by design: Creating a national and state standards-based high school science program. *The Science Teacher, 68*(7), 38–43.

Rule, A. C., Carnicelli, L. A., & Kane, S. S. (2004). Using poetry to teach about minerals in earth science class. *Journal of Geoscience Education, 52*(1), 10–14.

Sadker, M. P., & Sadker, D. M. (2005). *Teachers, schools, and society* (7th ed.). New York: McGraw-Hill.

Schulte, P. (1996). A definition of constructivism. *Science Scope, 19*(3), 25–27.

Scruggs, T. E., & Mastropieri, M. A. (1993). Current approaches to science education: Implications for mainstream instruction of students with disabilities. *Remedial and Special Education, 14*(1), 15–24.

Scruggs, T. E., & Mastropieri, M. A. (1995). Reflections on "Scientific reasoning of students with mild mental retardation: Investigating preconceptual and conceptual change." *Exceptionality, 5*(4), 249–257.

Scruggs, T. E., Mastropieri, M. A., & Wolfe, S. (1995). Scientific reasoning of students with mild mental retardation: Investigating preconceptual and conceptual change. *Exceptionality, 5*(4), 223–244.

Sharp, V. (2002). *Computer education for teachers: Integrating technology into classroom teaching* (4th ed.). New York: McGraw-Hill.

She, H.-C. (2005). Enhancing eighth grade students' learning of buoyancy: The interaction of teacher's instructional approach and students' learning preference styles. *International Journal of Science and Mathematics Education, 3*, 609–624.

Silverstein, S. (1996). Nope. In *Falling Up* (p. 17). New York: HarperCollins.

Smith, J. L., & Herring, J. D. (2001). *Using drama and literature to teach middle level content.* Portsmouth, NH: Heinemann.

Social Psychology Network. (2006). *Jigsaw classroom.* Retrieved November 13, 2006, from http://www.jigsaw.org

Stiffler, L. (1992). A solution in the shelves. *Science and Children, 29*(6), 17, 46.

Stocker, J. H. (1998). *Chemistry and science fiction.* Washington, DC: American Chemical Society.

Tatar, D., & Robinson, M. (2003). Use of the digital camera to increase student interest and learning in high school biology. *Journal of Science Education and Technology, 12*(2), 89–95.

Third International Mathematics and Science Study (TIMMS). (1996). A splintered vision: An investigation for U.S. mathematics and science education. East Lansing: U.S. National Research Center for the Third International Mathematics Study, Michigan State University.

Thompson, B. R., & MacDougall, G. D. (2002). Intelligent teaching. *The Science Teacher, 69*(1), 44–48.

Thompson, J. A. (2007). *Seeds for the future: The impact of genetically modified crops on the environment.* Ithaca, NY: Comstock.

Tierney, B. (with Dorroh, J.). (2004). *How to write to learn science* (2nd ed.). Arlington, VA: National Science Teachers Association Press.

Tobin, K., & Dawson, G. (1992). Constraints to curriculum reform: Teachers and the myths of schooling. *Education Technology, Research and Development, 40*(1), 81–92.

Vacca, R. T., & Vacca, J. L. (2005). *Content area reading: Literacy and learning across the curriculum.* Boston: Allyn & Bacon.

Versaci, R. (2001). How comic books can change the way our students see literature: One teachers' perspective. *English Journal, 91*(1), 61–67.

Wagner, E. J. (2006) *The science of Sherlock Holmes: From Baskerville Hall to the Valley of Fear, the real forensics behind the great detectives greatest cases.* Hoboken, NJ: John Wiley & Sons.

Wallen, E., Plass, J. L., & Brünken, R. (2005). The function of annotations in the comprehension of scientific texts: Cognitive lad effects and the impact of verbal ability. *Educational Technology Research and Development, 53*(3), 59–72.

Wandersee J., Mintzes, J., & Novak, J. (Eds.). (1998). *Learning science with understanding.* San Diego, CA: Academic Press.

Weiner, J. (1995). *The beak of the finch: A story of evolution in our time.* New York: Random House.

Wellington, J., & Osborne, J. (2001). *Language and literacy in science education.* Buckingham, UK: Open University Press.

Wiley, D., & Royce, C. (1999). *Investigate and connect. Earth and space science.* Grand Rapids, MI: Instructional Fair.

Williamson, K., Wright, S., Schauder, D., & Bow, A. (2001). The Internet for the blind and visually impaired. *Journal of Computer-Mediated Communication, 7*(1). Retrieved November 28, 2006, from http://www.ascisc.org

Willis, N. C. (2006). *Red knot: A shorebird's incredible journey.* Middleton, DE: Birdsong Books.

Wincbrenner, S. (1996). *Teaching kids with learning disabilities in the regular classroom: Strategies and techniques every teacher can use to challenge and motivate struggling students.* Minneapolis, MN: Free Spirit.

Wright, J. C., & Wright, C. S. (1998). A commentary on the profound changes envisioned by the National Science Standards. *Teachers College Record, 100*(1), 122–143.

Yolen, J. (1987). *Owl moon.* New York: Penguin.

Yolen, J. (1990). *Bird watch: A book of poetry.* New York: Penguin.

Yore, L. D., Hand, L., & Prain, B. M. (2002). Scientists as writers. *Science Education, 86,* 672–692.

Zigo, D., & Moore, M. T. (2004). Science fiction: Serious reading, critical reading. *English Journal, 94*(2), 85–90.

Index

Note: Page numbers followed by an intalicized *f* indicate figures.